Parenting Adhd

A Mindful Approach for Helping Your Child
Become Calm, Resilient, and Secure

(Deciding to Gradually Wean Your Toddler &
Making It Happen)

Kyle Williams

Published by Rob Miles

© **Kyle Williams**

All Rights Reserved

Parenting Adhd: A Mindful Approach for Helping Your Child Become Calm, Resilient, and Secure (Deciding to Gradually Wean Your Toddler & Making It Happen)

ISBN 9781990084386

All rights reserved. No part of this guide may be reproduced in any form without permission in writing from the publisher except in the case of brief quotations embodied in critical articles or reviews.

Legal & Disclaimer

The information contained in this book is not designed to replace or take the place of any form of medicine or professional medical advice. The information in this book has been provided for educational and entertainment purposes only.

The information contained in this book has been compiled from sources deemed reliable, and it is accurate to the best of the Author's knowledge; however, the Author cannot guarantee its accuracy and validity and cannot be held liable for any errors or omissions. Changes are periodically made to this book. You must consult your doctor or get professional medical advice before using any of the suggested remedies, techniques, or information in this book.

Upon using the information contained in this book, you agree to hold harmless the Author from and against any damages, costs, and expenses, including any legal fees potentially resulting from the application of any of the information provided by this guide. This disclaimer applies to any damages or injury caused by the use and application, whether directly or indirectly, of any advice or information presented, whether for breach of contract, tort, negligence, personal injury, criminal intent, or under any other cause of action.

You agree to accept all risks of using the information presented inside this book. You need to consult a professional medical practitioner in order to ensure you are both able and healthy enough to participate in this program.

Table of Contents

INTRODUCTION 1

CHAPTER 1: I'M NOT GOING TO LIE 2

CHAPTER 2: ENCOURAGING GOOD TODDLER BEHAVIOR .. 8

CHAPTER 3: "PROBLEM OR A GIFT": THE MAIN CHARACTER TRAITS OF A STRONG-WILLED CHILD 28

CHAPTER 4: JOYS OF PARENTHOOD 34

CHAPTER 5: BEFORE GETTING DOWN AND DIRTY – WHAT YOU NEED TO KNOW.. 44

CHAPTER 6: YOU AND YOUR TODDLER............................ 55

CHAPTER 7: LESSON ON RAISING HEALTHY KIDS 70

CHAPTER 8: MAN OR WOMAN: WHO IS A BETTER PARENT? 78

CHAPTER 9: ALARM BELLS 83

CHAPTER 10: TALKING TO YOUR CHILD SO THEY WILL REALLY 'LISTEN' 88

CHAPTER 11: CHALLENGE 2 – EMOTIONAL ADJUSTMENTS 93

- CHAPTER 12: IMPORTANCE OF CHILD DEVELOPMENT... 103
- CHAPTER 13: BE FIRM WITH AFFECTION.......................... 110
- CHAPTER 14: SINGLE DAD WITH A BABY: CHILD-PROOFING THE HOUSE.. 116
- CHAPTER 15: THE ARRIVAL: GAME IN SESSION.............. 124
- CHAPTER 17: HOW DO YOU CONNECT WITH YOUR TEENAGER? 145
- CHAPTER 18: MOTIVATING KIDS ON THEIR CHOICE OF LIFE THROUGH PROACTIVITY OVER REACTIVITY................... 150
- CHAPTER 19: GUIDELINES FOR BECOMING AN EFFECTIVE STEP PARENT.. 157
- CHAPTER 20: TRUTHS ABOUT SINGLE PARENT STATISTICS 161
- CHAPTER 21: TAKE CARE OF THEIR HEALTH................... 176
- CHAPTER 22: LIMITS AND RULES: WHEN YOU SHOULD TELL YOUR CHILD 'YES' AND 'NO' 181
- CONCLUSION... 197

Introduction

This book contains proven steps and strategies on how to raise your daughter into a confident girl.

This book will not only help you bring out the best from your daughter, but it will also be your guide in becoming a great parent for your young girl.

You will learn about the importance of self esteem in girls, women with self esteem then and now, the benefits your daughter could gain as she grows up with high regards to her self, and your role in boosting your daughter's confidence. This book will be the ultimate guide to helping your young girl gain the self esteem that she to succeed in today's world.

Let's begin.

Chapter 1: I'm not going to lie

I'm not going to lie, parenting is probably one of the hardest things anyone will ever have to do in their entire life. I'm actually pretty sure that it's not a secret at all, even if some people don't like to admit it. It's terrifying, and a lot of people naturally react to fear with anger or frustration. There's a little life in your hands, someone that counts on you to teach them everything about the world that they live in. A job that no one ever quite feels cut out for, the caretaker of innocence and a duty to prepare them to live in this world. A daunting task on its own, and even worse when sometimes you're working hard just to make ends meet.

We've all been there, staring at the stack of bills when approached with some kind of form or fee from the school, or even just allowance. We've been making dinner when the crash of a broken glass comes out of the next room and had to run out hoping that no one cut themselves. It's not exactly something anyone is prepared for, and it's easy to react with yelling and frustration to the stress that comes with it. Surprises happen every day of parenthood. In fact, I feel lucky when it's only one surprise a day that comes rushing at me.

But the most important thing to remember is that children learn how to deal with stress from their parents. Parents are the first to show a child how to react to the world around them. If the parents cope by yelling, they're going to learn those unhealthy habits too, but the good news is that we can still learn better ways, more productive ways to solve our problems and teach our children how to solve their problems in healthier ways too. Children look to their parents, they guide them as much as the outside world. Becoming better people helps set an example that being a decent human being is something that takes work and effort, but is very much worth doing.

It's been a long-held belief of mine that one of the important ways we can give a healthier world to our children is to give healthier children to the world, to clarify, I don't mean physical health, though that would be a great thing to do. I'm talking about raising future adults with healthy mental states and the ability to cope effectively with new and stressful situations. Kids that react well under stress and contribute in a positive manner to the rest of society.

One of the major solutions is to build trust in the child. The child has to learn to trust, trust in themselves to solve problems and trust in their parents to help them figure out how to solve issues that they may have. It's a trust that isn't easy to form, especially if it's a goal that's set with an older child rather than a younger one.

The techniques I'm presenting may make it seem simple, but they require time and patience. There is no truly simple solution, no right answer to the problems in the world. No one is going to get it right immediately. Mistakes will be made, and that's fine. It's alright to make mistakes, what's important is learning constantly. Each technique is going to take some customization to each unique family situation, so don't be afraid to step outside of the box and find a way to build a healthier family.

I'm a parent myself. I understand the challenges that come from raising kids, and even raising kids is a permanent learning process. It's alright if you don't have it all right. No one ever does, even the perfect looking parents you see. Kids aren't perfect. Parents aren't perfect. We all have more to learn. The biggest mistake in parenting is thinking that we know everything about it, that there's nothing more to learn. Nothing to surprise us anymore. Nothing that we can get wrong. If we allow ourselves to get into that kind of mindset that is when we've failed as parents. As long as you haven't gotten to that point, you can still improve and become a better person and a better person. The fact that you're still reading books like this means that you care enough to keep trying to learn things to help your children and you should be applauded. A lot of it comes down just trying your best to be a decent human being in your day to day life, but even that takes effort and sometimes everyone needs advice on the matter. Don't be afraid to question and form opinions, to see what works for you and your family and modify any of the ideas presented here. My family is not yours. I cannot know what works best for you, only some basic general principles that work for most people with modification to specific family situations and specific children needs. Each child is different and may respond different ways to different parenting techniques, even within the same family.

It's important to keep your child's unique needs in mind. There is no single solution to every family, but many of the basics translate between them.

But that's enough of a soapbox for me, let's get into some actual techniques. It is possible to bring more positivity to your family. It's worth all the work.

Chapter 2: Encouraging Good Toddler Behavior

One of the most effective ways to encourage positive behavior in children is through praise. Children seek love and recognition for their efforts and progress. Praise increases children's self-confidence and motivation by making them feel happy. It is important to give them confidence in their abilities and to show them that they feel proud when they behave correctly, thereby encouraging good behavior. Here are some highly effective tips to help encourage positive behavior.

Encourage Effort

Use praise to encourage effort and to enhance the progress of your child. A child who can use the bathroom alone for the first time or perform a task that he was not able to do before deserves recognition. In this way, it is encouraging the child's development and autonomy.

Reinforce Attitudes

Enjoy instilling some values that you consider fundamental, important, and positive. By praising and reinforcing attitudes, you help to develop social skills that will make relationships easier in the future.

Praise the Effort, Regardless of the Result

The effort must be praised even if the goal is not fully achieved. If your child did not receive an excellent grade, but studied and worked for this to be possible, it is important to recognize him. Praise is key to staying motivated and therefore improving your bottom line.

Praise Good Behavior

It is important to praise good behavior; do not save compliments only for great achievements. Small behavior improvements should also be valued. If we only pay attention at times where behavior needs work, children will feel inclined to do wrong.

Approve or Disregard Attitudes and Not the Child

As much as you consider your child to be very handsome, intelligent, etc., avoid telling him this often. This type of label turns out to be as harmful as the opposite ("you're dumb," "you're bad," etc.). Try to mark your approval or disapproval regarding attitudes, not the child.

Value the Achievements of the Family

It is important to value the achievements and efforts of the family. If a brother has conquered something, it is important to praise him, as well, the achievements of the father or mother. It is important to recognize the effort of all the elements and celebrate the achievements in the family.

Rewards

You can also choose to reward your child, such as a gift, a trip to the movies, or candy if you want to reinforce an attitude. But do not make it a routine, because this can lead to only good behavior when rewarded. Most behavior should be rewarded only by praise. Also, you may be tempted to use the allowance as a reward. We do not recommend it. Never use the allowance to "buy" your child.

Rewarding the child for good behavior teaches them to understand that there is a direct link between action and consequence.

Remember that as a parent you are a role model for your children. It is essential that you be a good role model by providing them with appropriate rules and standards to follow. Consistency is the key. Children learn by observing others, and they will learn these qualities. With a little persuasion and positive reinforcement, you can teach, encourage, and create positive behavior in children.

How To Stimulate Good Behavior In Children

Educating our children was not easy. So I went after tips on how to encourage good behavior in children without having to punish and scold every second.

Stimulating good behavior in children is one of the best ways to impose limits, without having to apply punishments constantly. The only problem is how to do that. In most cases, our little ones tested our limits and seem to do anything not to obey.

Here are ways to stimulate good behavior:

Be The Example

Being an example is the most effective way we have to teach our children anything - both good and bad. When it comes to encouraging good behavior in children, it is no different. Here are a few examples of what you can do for your child to learn.

Catch your child's attention when you split snacks with your husband or when you have to wait in the bank queue, pointing out that adults also have to share and wait too.

Realize The Good Behavior

If you are like any parent in the world when your child is behaving well, you leave him playing alone and take advantage of the time to do anything you may need to. But when your child is behaving badly, you direct all your attention to him to resolve the situation. Your attention is what kids most want, so to get this attention sometimes children will behave badly. The best way to encourage good behavior in children is to pay attention when they are behaving well and to take your attention from them when they are behaving badly. This is completely counter-intuitive for us and can be a difficult habit to cultivate. But once you get used to it, it will become easier and easier.

A great way to do this is to play with your child when he is quiet in his corner and praise him when he obeys you the first time you speak.

Understand The Stage Of Development

This tip is easy to understand. Each child has a behavior; however, you cannot require a child of three to act as the same as a child who is ten. That is, do not try to go to a three-hour lunch with your little boy hoping he will be quiet for the whole lunch. Do not want a two-year-old child not to put everything in his mouth. Each age has a phase, and it is no use wanting to demand different behavior from a child.

Have Appropriate Expectations

This is a continuation of the above tip. Parents have high expectations. This is not wrong when expectations are possible. For example, do not expect a tired child to behave well, or a one-month-old baby to sleep through the night.

Create Structure and Routine

A child with a structured routine tends to behave better. They already know what to expect and are used to it. A child with a routine feels safe and thus lives more calmly. A child without a routine has a sense of insecurity that will disrupt much in the time to educate and encourage good behavior.

Uses Disciplinary Strategies

Rather than humiliating or beating children, there are positive disciplinary strategies that teach, set boundaries, and encourage good behavior in children. Some of these are: give options, put somewhere to think, talk, give affection and a system of rewards (reward can be a simple compliment, it does not have to be gifts or food).

Understand That The Bad Behavior Worked So Far

If throwing tantrums and disobeying worked for him to get your attention so far, changing this behavior will take time. He will have to realize and understand that you will no longer pay attention to him when he behaves badly, but when he behaves well.

Instilling good behavior practices in young children is a must for any responsible parent, but sometimes it can also be quite complicated and laborious. However, beginning to instill this type of behavior as early as possible will help build a good foundation for the child's behavior and attitudes in the future. It is necessary to be aware that in the first years of life the children are like "sponges" and results will be better if you begin to show them early and direct them to appropriate behaviors of life in society.

Here are some more ideas to help parents with the task of encouraging good behavior in their children.

Models To Follow

Children tend to mirror the behaviors of parents and those with whom they coexist more closely. Therefore, be careful about your behaviors and language used when the child is around to avoid misunderstanding ideas and misconceptions about how you should behave towards others. This includes talking properly and behaving politely to both your partner and family, as well as to the child. Try to avoid loud, unstructured arguments when the child is around. We do not mean you can't disagree with your spouse, because the child must also be aware that these exist. But try to have the arguments always controlled and civil around children.

Be Firm

Parents should be affectionate, but still adamant about instilling discipline in their children. It is important that the child knows how to respect his parents, even when he does not have what he wants. Understanding when to say "no" at the right times is an important step in your education.

Positive Body Language

Your body language has a huge impact when you are trying to instill a particular behavior in children. Given the height of the child, a parent standing while correcting the errors and applying discipline is often viewed as authoritative. It is advisable to place yourself at the same level as the child's eyes. Sit next to the child while talking to them and always maintain eye contact.

Establishing Limits

It is fundamental to establish limits, rules, and consequences for unwanted behavior. Increase limits on children to be able to distinguish right from wrong. They need to know what is not acceptable and clear reasons that make it wrong so that there is no doubt in the child's mind about the behavior to adopt.

You started tracking your child's progress long before he left the warmth of your belly: in the tenth week, the heart began beating; on the 24th week, his hearing developed and listened to your voice; in the 30th week, he began to prepare for childbirth. Now that he or she is in your arms, you're still eager to keep up with all the signs of your little one's development and worries that he might be left behind. Nonsense! Excessive worry will not help at all, so take your foot off the accelerator and enjoy each phase. Your child will realize all the fundamental achievements of maturity. He will learn to walk, talk, potty, and when you least expect it, you will be riding a bicycle alone (and no training wheels!). He will do all only in his time.

Stop taking developmental milestones so seriously. For example, your 7-month-old son will be able to sit alone and at age 3 will be able to ride a tricycle. Consider what is expected for each age just for reference. The best thing to do is to set aside the checklist of the abilities your child needs to develop and play together a lot. There is no better way to connect with and develop your child than through playtime.

To help you even further in realizing the goals mentioned above or processes, I would like to mention some tips here that stimulate a child's intellectual, motor, social, and emotional development:

Rainbow

The baby starts noticing colors at around 3 months of age when the vision is no longer so blurry. That is why, at this age, the idea is to stimulate with strong colors, which can be in toys or mobile in the crib. Babies also love contrast: you can see that stripes are not missing in children's toys. At about a year and a half, your child will begin to notice the difference between one color and another, even if he does not know the color's name. So, start saying: "Let's play with that blue ball" or "Take the red tomato from the salad." This way colors become part of their day to day life.

Books

The role of parents is fundamental for children to learn to love reading and to make books a pleasure, rather than an obligation. According to the latest edition of the Portraits of Reading survey in Brazil, for 43% of readers, the mother was the main influence for developing the desire for reading, and for 17%, the father was the one who played the role. From the third month of your child's life, you can use plastic books in the bath. From the sixth, when the baby can already carry objects to the mouth with his hands, leave cloth books in the cradle - in addition to being able to bite them, he will not be able to rip the pages! At all ages, talk about the cover, the pictures, the colors and let the child turn the pages.

Memory

Memory is a form of storing knowledge and must be permeated by a context. Start by helping your child memorize words by showing a represented object. If you are walking on the street and crossing a bicycle, point and say, "Look, son, a bicycle." This is how he will build associations. From the first year, he will say a few words and try to repeat the names of what you show. But it is from the age of 2 that the ability to retain information increases.

Creating

Create characters and a dream of fantastic worlds. All of this is important in developing the creativity of little ones; it also contributes to problem-solving. To make the narrative more exciting, how about testing the improvisational ability of the two of you? Separate figures from objects, landscapes, colors, foods, and animals – they can be drawn or cut from magazines. While one narrates, the other can select images that portray elements that should be included in the narrative. The challenge is to be able to fit them together so that the narrative continues to make sense. By age 7, as the child is already literate, you can help him record your adventures in small booklets.

Always Ask

When picking up your child from school, you say, "How was your day?" And he says, "Cool." It was not exactly what you wanted to hear, right? To avoid generic responses, develop the questions so that the child needs to express what he thinks and justify his response. Ask: "What did you enjoy most today?" And he will be forced to develop more elaborate reasoning, requiring him to work linguistic and logical skills. At 3 years old, he can already relate experiences he went through and say whether those were good or bad. At 4, you can ask for details, descriptions, and names of colleagues who were with him.

Blessed Doubt

"Why does a dog not eat pizza?" "Was Grandma Ever a Child?" Although child questioning can make adults uncomfortable or embarrassed, these are essential for understanding the child's world. It is the process of distinguishing between real and imaginary (which occurs around the age of 4) and the construction of relations between known elements. That's why the "why questions" are so important in the child's development process. Even if you do not know how to respond to everything your child asks, show that his or her concern is relevant, and recognize when you do not know the answer.

Play, Clean, Play

As your child plays, insist that he engage in one game at a time, to build concentration. "Do you not want to play bowling anymore?" From age 2, your child can help clean up the toy he was using, before picking up a new one, so he also develops the sense of organization.

Belly-Down

Your child begins to strengthen the body between the first and the sixth month. Because thick motor development (involving the activities of large muscles such as sitting and walking) occurs in the head to toe direction, the first step is to strengthen the neck muscles. Beginning the first month, give your child at least two periods a day supported belly downtime on a flat and firm surface. In this way, the baby can lean securely and lift his head. At 6 months, he will start to sit alone. Arrange several cushions around him to help him get stronger.

Clap, Clap, Tum, Tum

One of the best ways to develop motor coordination is to teach rhythm to your child. To do this, just use your hands. From the seventh month, clap with him to the sounds of your favorite songs, interspersing slow songs with other accelerated songs, so he can see the difference. You will see that your baby will be able to hit his little hands.

Everything Fits

From the age of 7 months, the baby begins to hold objects; in about a year and a half, he will begin to put pieces together. Besides being a good exercise for coordination, the child will learn which part will fit within the other. For your child to enjoy and learn from this, he can play with pots and plastic mugs while you prepare lunch. From the age of two and a half, also offer small puzzles (about six pieces).

Step By Step

Climbing stairs is a great exercise to develop agility and coarse motor coordination, as well as assisting to strengthen muscles. At 1 year of age, the child can already perform the activity, but only by placing both feet on the same step, one at a time. With growth, he will gain strength and balance until by age 3, he will probably rise by placing one foot on each step alternately. Even at this stage, it is important that he be accompanied by an adult to avoid accidents.

Bonding & Trust

Establishing relationships of trust is important for the development of the child. The first people he does it with are the parents. For this, one factor is essential: never lie. If the child goes to the doctor to take a vaccine, do not even think about saying that you are just going for a walk. If he asks if the injection will hurt, be honest and say it will, yes, but it will pass. The experts are all in agreement: explain everything. Tell him he's going to get wet, it's going to hurt, he's going to be cold, so he knows what to expect and learns to trust what you say.

Congratulate your child when he is good at something, encouraging him to continue. If scolding is necessary, pay close attention to how to do it. Saying "what you did was naughty" is quite different from saying "you are naughty!" Do not let the child think that the criticized trait is part of his personality, so he will not incorporate this trait into his self-image.

Chapter 3: "Problem Or A Gift": The Main Character Traits Of A Strong-Willed Child

Most people view strong-willed children as problematic. You can see this in the rather harsh adjectives used to describe such children, including but not limited to:

Picky

Demanding

Stubborn

Wayward

Domineering

Difficult

Obstinate

Disobedient

Unruly

Naughty

Rebellious

Capricious

The thing most people miss about these "problematic" traits in children is that they are the same traits celebrated in adults. A rebel who defies the rules makes a great CEO or civil rights activist. An unruly young man with anger problems makes a great athlete when he learns to channel his aggression into a sport. A capricious woman challenges the status quo and brings about change within an organization. All of the celebrities, entrepreneurs, Olympic athletes, and world leaders you admire have these same traits, which is how they achieved what they have today.

Once a strong-willed child becomes an adult, those negative traits that he was shamed for in childhood now become more positive ones:

Determined

Perseverant

Dedicated

Strong

Confident

Firm

Decisive

Therefore, is your strong-willed child really a problem? Or has he been born with a gift? The answer is that your child's difficult traits are actually great ones. They just add challenges to your parenting. Being able to appreciate your child's gifts, instead of treating them as a problem, will enable you to become a more positive parent. Looking at your child in this new light will influence your behavior subconsciously, and in turn your relationship with your child will rapidly take a turn for the better without too much effort on your part. However, you should also make a conscious effort to celebrate and praise your child's strengths and show him how to use his gifts for good instead of bad. These actions and attitude adjustments will lead to a world of difference.

Let's look at what strong-willed children are capable of to further realize what gifts they have.

The first is creativity. They think differently than others and have to ask questions or find new ways of doing things, which can be misconstrued as obstinacy.

They are passionate and tackle what they care about with vivacity.

They have scientific minds and must inquire "Why?" all the of the time, and they are not satisfied with banal answers.

They are self-sufficient and learn on their own from their experiences. They must experience new things to grow, even if they have been told not to have those experiences by adults in their lives.

They demand perfection of themselves and others. They need things just right.

They demand a lot of praise to keep their confidence up. Sometimes, they seek a lot of reassurance as they form their personalities.

They are so passionate that they demand to be heard.

They become hyper focused on one area or project of interest, dedicating everything to it and neglecting their chores or homework.

They hate doing things that they see no point in doing; the frivolous and banal does not interest them because they see the bigger picture and tasks of more importance.

They make their own decisions and stand by them. From an early age, they have a high level of independence and the ability to lead their own lives with minimal guidance.

All of these behaviors can be difficult to contend with in a child because they indicate a child is not willing to just do whatever you want. You will butt heads with a child who displays these tendencies. But congratulations, your child has many gifted abilities that will make him a super successful adult. Recognize that these stubborn or obstinate behaviors are signs of intelligence, inquiry, and independence, the traits of a true leader.

Chapter 4: Joys Of Parenthood

To be honest, there are many days when parenting is far from joy. From the child going manic and out of control at the supermarket, to the teen on drugs, to the child that refuses to study, right to the child that is hell-bent on having the most destructive identity, we can all agree that some days parenting is anything but joy (okay now that we have been honest, let's continue).

But in times of despair and frustration, we must remember the joys of parenthood and focus on our love and memories of joy. This simple act of focusing on the positive aspects of parenthood allows us to re-program our minds and put things back into the proper perspective. So this book will start out by putting things back into perspective (the major cause of emotional turmoil for parents of strong-willed kids is a complete loss of perspective).

For mothers, childbirth is an emotional rollercoaster. Through nine months of pregnancy, they are plagued with worrying thoughts: Will it be a boy or a girl? What will they be like? What does their future hold? But as soon as the time comes for birth, the worry seems to melt away—as soon as the child is placed in the arms of their mother, she seldom feels a greater sense of purpose and fulfillment. In fact, it's the act of becoming a parent that many people say is the most joyful act in their lives. Raising a child, whether as a single parent or as a couple, can be both rewarding and challenging for mothers and fathers.

After childbirth, priorities quickly change and suddenly, your child is the most important thing to you. Selflessness kicks in, and it's no longer your future you're worrying about, but rather theirs. Your wish is to protect them from the dangers and uncertainty of the world and instead, provide a sense of safety and comfort, offering guidance and advice that will help to instill good values and the ability to make the right choices in difficult situations. In short, when you become a parent, it's no longer about your needs, as they come second to the care and wellbeing of your child.

If you have dreams or goals in life, reaching them becomes necessary. They become important, not only to provide for your family but to inspire and set a good example for your child. You often see many children follow in their parent's footsteps, even entering the same career field once they've grown. They were inspired to be successful by witnessing the passion their parents showed in the same situation, whether it was becoming a doctor, a lawyer, an athlete or nearly any other profession, including being a parent themselves.

Despite the overwhelming love and affection many parents feel for their new-born baby, not all parents embrace the birth of a child with the same level of joy. In some cases, babies are unexpected or unplanned. Perhaps the parents are too young to care for another life or are unwilling to put the children ahead of themselves. Whatever the case, caring and providing for a child is hard no matter what, but the reward of seeing your child grow into a loving and caring person makes all your sacrifices worthwhile.

Needless to say, those who are willing to embrace parenting in all it has to offer have so much to look forward to and enjoy.

Even though parents must make sacrifices for their children, it is an even trade-off. The intense feeling of love and joy in caring for a child is rare and something that cannot be found elsewhere—there are simply no words that can describe just how beautiful a baby is. Parents get satisfaction from providing for their child and feel good when they see them reach a new milestone. It becomes so easy to share and revel in their achievements, even from as early as day one. From a baby learning to crawl to its first steps and first words, like "mama" and "da-da", these little moments are the reward for all the hard work. Many parents find themselves recording these moments for posterity, and looking back on them when their child is older. In these videos or photographs, you will likely see or hear pure joy of the parents as their pride just cannot be contained. This is the best representation of the joys of parenting.

Examples of the Joys of Parenthood

The First Night after Your Baby Is Born

The day of childbirth can be overwhelming and hectic. From the constant flow of doctors, nurses and visitors to the hours of labor, it can leave you feeling pretty burnt out. But after the chaos has died down and when a mother is left alone with her baby, one-on-one, that's the moment that it sets in, a bond of a feeling of unconditional love for this new life we have brought into this world.

When Your Child Begins to Communicate with You

As soon as your child starts to talk to you, an instant bond is created, even deeper than you experienced with them before. Not only does communication make providing for them so much easier, but also they are able to give feedback to your words. Even their smiling back at something you said can be a powerful realization that your baby is growing into an intelligent little person and only getting smarter as time passes. When they can begin to have small conversations with you and express their likes and dislikes, their personality will truly shine. It's in these stages that your relationship grows, and you may even find out they're like you in more ways than you know.

When Your Child Begins to Walk

Every parent dreams of seeing their child take their first steps or better yet, recording that very moment. There is often such a great sense of pride as we watch our children take their first steps towards independence and development.

When Your Child Learns New Skills

Walking is just the beginning of a series of new and incredible skills your baby will learn at what might seem like lightning fast speed. Once a baby is healthy and energetic enough, they won't want to stay in one place.

Watching a child develop mobility curiosity and intelligence is a very rewarding experience for parents.

But this natural part of a child's development can also be a be bittersweet experience for many parents who wish they could hold on to their baby just a little longer.

When Your Child Tells You "I Love You."

Children are better listeners than you might think. The words you say to your child are soaked up and begin to register meaning in their minds. When you tell your child that you love them, they sense that it's something good, especially when it's followed by a kiss on the cheek. In no time at all, when your child is a toddler, you will be surprised and overcome with emotion when you hear the response to something you've said a million times— "I love you, too." It will be sure to leave a lasting smile on your face, and it is a moment you won't soon forget.

Successes of Your Child

Parents are always telling their children "I'm proud of you", and they really are. No matter how many times it is said, it never loses meaning. Imagine being out with friends and other parents watching your child's football game and your child scores a touchdown. You don't just jump for joy because they may win the game, but instead because it's a sign that your child is fully capable of doing anything they can imagine. Containing the excitement in these situations is hard. The same applies to other successes, like starring in a school play, singing in the choir or doing well in a science fair or other academic achievements. The more your child learns and grows, the more opportunities they afford themselves in life. It's through these opportunities that they find more and more success, and these successes bring you joy as a parent because it reminds you just how far you and your child have come. It makes you proud and joyful to raise a child to become a successful adult and all around good person.

Many other instances and occasions create joy as a parent, including the following:

Watching your child on the playground

Cuddling with your baby

Funny conversations or questions

When they tell you that you are the best

Watching them gain their independence

Holding your hand as you walk

Playing with them and reliving your own childhood Calming their fears of nightmares or monsters

Knowing they'll always be part of you

When they learn to do things they love, like swim, dance, draw, paint, etc.

Witnessing all of their firsts

Receiving love and trust in return

The joy of parenting is about living in the moment. If you are mindful of the gift that a child is, your relationship with them will be strengthened. It's all about enjoying time with your children and appreciating them for who they are in the present. It boosts their self-esteem and makes you feel great, too. Not all parent-child relationships are superb, however. Parents aren't perfect, and there are many reasons that some relationships become strained and cause adverse effects on the children. It's important to create a safe and loving environment for your child and doing so will nurture and grow your relationship so you can experience all the amazing moments of joy in raising a child, even if they are strong-willed and challenging to raise.

Chapter 5: Before Getting Down And Dirty – What You Need To Know

Kids are cuddly and cute beings that seem to live in the land of marshmallows and rainbows – that is if you only see them on social networking sites. Try to spend a full week with babies and you'll see a very different side. Babies can be very demanding, unpredictable, can scream for hours at length, and inconsolably at a whim. And they do this every single day for the first few months that it will affect how you function both mentally and emotionally. But the good news is, people survive it. Maybe it's the power of love, or maybe it's the human spirit. Either way, being a parent remains to be one of the most fulfilling roles that you can take, and one of the craziest (not to mention longest) rides to embark in.

While no book or advice can ever fully prepare you, the following are some of the most important things to keep in mind before entering a life of parenthood. Bear in mind that parenting is not just about how you handle the diapers and how you take care of them when they're already there; it is also about how you take care of yourself and how you get ready to become the best parent that you can be for your precious ones. Just like in war, it always pays to be ready before hitting the battleground!

It's not always easy to get pregnant

Some people keep off pregnancy for many years thinking that when they finally decide to have kids, they can just have sex every day for a month and the baby will follow. This isn't always a case. All orally taken or injected birth control methods should be stopped months before you try to conceive, because these can alter the ovulation cycle of a woman's body.

The health of the woman is also important not just during pregnancy, but also when planning to conceive. The chances of pregnancy decrease with increasing body weight, and worsen when the woman smokes. Taking multivitamins are also highly recommended, to make up for the lost nutrients. Folic acid is one of the key supplements that are required at least a month prior conception, and at least 12 weeks during the pregnancy.

Time is of the essence, especially when considering the biological clock of women. Most studies say that 85% get pregnant within a year of trying, but the situation changes for women nearing 30. Rate of conception declines from 25 to 30 years of age, and suffers a steeper decline when a woman hits 35. Couples must rethink before putting off pregnancy if the woman is no longer in their 20's because of this. Late pregnancies also increase the risk of disorders on the conceived child.

It's always best to consult your doctor during the planning stages of the pregnancy for close guidance on what to eat and what to take. This helps you to ensure a healthy and safe pregnancy which will definitely work for you and your child.

To Quit or Not to Quit My Job?

This is one of the most important decisions to be made before having a child. Taking care of a baby is a 24/7 role, and there are pros and cons of having a nanny. Sit down and talk to your partner if one of you is willing to give up their jobs for the kids. Countries like Canada, Albania, Denmark, and UK are blessed to have a full year of allowable maternity leave while most other countries only allow for three to four months.

Here are some questions that may guide how you make that decision. These can apply both when you have a partner and when you are a single mom.

• How much do you and your partner really earn? First things first, you have to be honest about what you have and what you don't have.

•Are you willing to drastically reduce your lifestyle to reduce your expenses? This needs to go beyond the rhetorical, you have to project your budget without a job and really list down the cost of your expenses versus your cash flow. This will help to make you visualize how quitting your job can affect your lifestyle and the extent of your spending.

• Are you willing to take work-at-home or freelance jobs to supplement your earnings? There are so many options online and this is a route that most moms take when wanting to be a stay-at-home mom.

• Can you work on a compromise? More often than not, it can be very hard to let go of your job, most especially when you're at the peak of your career. Consider talking to your superior for options of a more flexible job schedule, or probably a less demanding line of work. Some companies can allow for this kind of setup.

At one point in motherhood, there will be a time when you will definitely be itching to be a fulltime mom and devote all your time to your kids. Being there for them 24/7 is one of the best ways to rear emotionally healthy children, as will be discussed in the succeeding chapters; however one must never forget to take practical considerations before taking this route. This entails a huge risk, but it also reaps great parenting rewards.

Healthcare coverage

The importance of healthcare coverage must be stressed especially in countries where insurance is not popular, or for people who think that healthcare coverage is just like throwing money away. Much of the family budget, especially for families that are still starting out, is dedicated to the baby's needs. Either of the parents getting sick is an unwelcome surprise and tends to drain the budget that is already allocated to other matters.

Some healthcare coverage's allow their dependents to be covered up to the age of 26, so this means if you're still below this age limit, you can use the health care of your parents for emergency situations, but beyond this you're on your own. Make sure to examine how much is covered by your healthcare plan before subscribing to one. Getting yourself covered is a responsible way of ensuring that you have your children covered too.

Let loose and do everything you've always dreamed of

When the kid is there, it will no longer be about you – for a long time at least. Life will revolve around your little bosses. Do something spontaneous, have a lot of fun! Why not try the following suggestions?

•Have your dream vacation, and take a lot of photos – If you are dreaming of that one exotic place to bathe in the sun, take on your dream adventure or just roll in the sand, now is the time to do it! When you finally have kids, vacations will mean constantly worrying if junior will trip on a rock or what your little princess is constantly munching in her other hand.

Take out your life-checklist and try to tick off as many items as possible. The idea is to get as many life experiences as you possibly can, and have something to remember them by. Do this so that at one point in your life, when you find your baby screaming like the world is about to end, you haven't done the dishes, the house is a mess, and you realize you've forgotten to cook – you can hold on to something that reminds you of how awesome a person you are, and that yes, you will survive.

On a side note, investing on a good camera will also give you great photos of your pregnancy and all your little tots' firsts. Children grow so fast so you better make the most out of those precious moments.

•Get as much sleep as you possibly can – This is probably not the first time that you've heard how taking care of a baby means being awake every two hours in the evening until you start looking like a zombie. So yes, stock up on a lot of sleep. Not that you can actually 'stock on' sleep but it helps to remember that at least you were able to enjoy it while you can.

•Get awfully drunk, and get stupid – because when you finally have children, you will not always be able to do this out in the open. Being a parent also includes the pressure of being a 'role model', so whether you like it or not, you will have to act more responsibly.

•Have mind-blowing sex – Yes and do it often. That position you saw on the magazine? Go try it! Shower your partner with all that naughty attention. When your little one is born, there will be months of rare or no sex at all because you're both either too tired and you just want to catch up on sleep. It's normal for women to lose sex drive months after giving birth - before you panic, don't worry, it'll come back.

Address your emotional baggage

Every person has a past, something that they fiercely hold on to or something they may be struggling to forget. It may be a traumatic experience, a deep-seated insecurity, or sudden bouts of depression. Either way, negative emotion that is hidden for too long will come haunting you in the future, and will definitely affect your children. In the same way that anything unpleasant happening in the house, regardless if its daddy's or mommy's fault, will always bring more damage to the young ones.

Do address any long term struggles that you've had that you feel is troubling you.

Talk about it with your partner, and if needed, seek for professional help. Keep in mind that if you are troubled, your children will get affected too, and you will not be able to hide it for very long.

When flying a plane, what do you think is the wisdom behind instructing you to put on your oxygen mask first before assisting your children? This is because as a universal rule, you must take care of yourself first before you are able to take care of others. Love yourself so you'd have enough love to give your family. This is the first half of parenting – getting yourself, your body, your heart, and your soul ready for it. Isn't this exciting?

Chapter 6: You And Your Toddler

Parent Self Care

Without a doubt, parenting is a full time job. But like any other occupation, all parents also need some **'time off'** to be able to have hope of doing a decent job of rearing a child. Parenting burnout often occurs when normal coping mechanisms become overwhelmed and parents becomes emotionally exhausted, making them incapable of nurturing and enforcing authority on a child. Suffice it to say, this is a point where the very pleasure and joy of parenting no longer exists, but instead it is regarded as a burden where parents feel the need to escape.

Parents of young children are more vulnerable to burnout mainly because of the mental, emotional and physical workload of raising a toddler. This developmental phase means more diapers, more toys, more laundry, more crying, more talking and more tantrums to pacify.

As a parent, it is a normal instinct to prioritize the needs of your child. When they were infants, you immediately respond to their cries, and as they grow older, you have grown more vigilant in their safety and development of their skills. In view of all these parenting demands and challenges, it's all too easy to lose track of your own self.

However, it is important to keep in mind that a crucial part of caring for your child is caring for your own self. While it is important to constantly keep track of what your toddler needs, it should not obscure your personal needs and that of your entire family. Most parents find themselves in a state of near exhaustion. It shouldn't have to be that way.

Truth is, it is impossible to nurture your child if there is nothing left to give. Hence, it is vital for parents to also look after themselves. Here are some helpful tips to cope and fight off exhaustion:

1. Take mini-breaks. Taking short breaks during the day while your child is occupied or asleep will give you time to rest and be refreshed to face the rest of the day. Additionally, occasional night outs and weekend getaways can also work wonders in recharging your batteries.

2. Don't lose your humor. Being a parent is not an all-serious lifestyle. Have a laugh, it is a great coping mechanism and provides you better perspective on things. By all means, go ahead and watch a funny movie or do some crazy stuff with your kid.

3. Share the load. Child rearing doesn't have to be the sole responsibility of mothers. If you constantly find yourself doing everything around the house, start delegating other responsibilities to your partner. This includes sharing the discipline and childcare workload.

4. Build a support group. Raising a child is difficult, especially if you have isolated yourself. Having solid social connections that will provide a steady flow of support will make the parenting journey more bearable and enjoyable.

5. Manage your guilt. Some parents deal with guilt problems when leaving their child with a babysitter or taking naps during the day. This is an irrational worry that will only help you work yourself into a burnout.

Remember, as a parent, you deserve to have days away from your child, for the sake of your sanity and well-being. If you feel you are on a brink of a burnout, take a serious look at how you run your life and determine what changes to be made to help you regain the joy and pleasure of being a parent.

The Chemistry of Attachment

Babies are born helpless, constantly needing to be cared for and protected at all times. However, from birth, the infant's brain synapses and hormonal control system start to permanently organize based on the human interactions he or she encounters day to day.

The interaction between a child and parents has been widely considered as a crucial influence on the proper function and development of a child. These powerful influences include personality formation, behavior, empathy and academic achievement. In fact, the relationship between parent and child is the most important factor in the development and behavior of the child.

Oxytocin, the Bonding Hormone

Oxytocin is a chemical released by the brain as a response to social interaction, most especially with skin-to-skin contact. This substance is also known to promote bonding patterns and promotes a natural desire for further contact. Oxytocin is found to multiply dramatically among expecting mothers, effectively increasing maternal behaviors and instincts.

Consistent and regular body contact as well as other nurturing acts by parents result in a constant elevated level of oxytocin in toddlers. This significantly lowers the child's stress hormone responses, making the child more "**securely attached**". A number of psychology studies have demonstrated that lack of parental bond results in "**insecure**" characteristics, which can trigger aggression, anti-social behavior as well as poor handling of stress.

Vasopressin and Protection

While this particular hormone is present during mother and toddler bonding, vasopressin plays an equally important role in fathers. This particular hormone is responsible for promoting brain reorganization for enhancing paternal behaviors, making fathers more dedicated and protective of his partner and child. Thus, it has been tagged as the "monogamy hormone".

Prolactin and Behavior

Prolactin plays a very important role in maintaining immune and reproductive organ function. This hormone is released during sleep. It is also known to promote care-giving behavior. According to studies, prolactin hormones are released among fathers in response to threats, whereas childless and single males do not. With prolonged elevation of this hormone, intimate and loving family relationships are sustained.

Spending quality time with toddlers is not only beneficial for children, but it also helps forge a loving and nurturing relationship of the whole family. But with all the fancy toys and gadgets readily available today, it can be quite a challenge competing for your child's attention. Here are some great ideas to make bonding time with your toddler more meaningful:

1. Do puzzles together

2. Make phone calls to other family members.

3. Visit a pet store or aquarium.

4. Read books together.

5. Sing songs and dance with your kid.

Toddlers find security in routines. Thus, it is important to establish small day-to-day activities, such as singing a special song together before bedtime or making Mickey Mouse pancakes every Sunday. This will turn a simple bonding moment into a special tradition that will help you feel closer to your child.

Your toddler expects their parents to provide stability and structure in their lives. By providing physical and emotional needs, such as playing and cuddling on a regular basis, the parental bond is strengthened. Children raised in loving and stable homes are known to grow up as loving and stable adults.

The Golden Rules of Positive Parenting

Positive parenting encompasses all aspects of child rearing—from learning to become more patient to firmly setting limits.

Parenting style shape a child's development, perception, behavior as well as their relationships with other people.

By being a positive parent, you will be able to nurture the growth and development of your toddler by establishing a stable, supportive and respectful relationship. Here are some positive parenting techniques to help you get started:

1. Take time to understand your child's behavior. Instead of merely reacting to a certain behavior or action, take time to understand and empathize with why your toddler is behaving in a particular way. This will help you formulate a more effective and appropriate response.

2. Be a more proactive parent. Instead of constantly correcting misbehavior, find opportunities to prevent it from happening. For example, you have observed your toddler to throw a royal fit when tired or hungry. This means, you need to make sure you provide ample rest and healthy snacks throughout the day.

Remember, avoiding certain situations that trigger misbehavior means winning half the battle.

3. Instill discipline with love. Toddlers feel more secure and safe when parents establish clear and defined limits for behavior. The positive parenting approach is setting limits with love and respect, and consistently enforcing them. Take time to properly set and establish the rules and inform your child of the consequences in advance. Follow through when you feel necessary.

4. Laugh often and much. Parenting is not all about restrictions and discipline. Be sure that both of you as parents have fun with your child as often as possible. Go out of your way to enjoy your toddler's company, such as playing a game together or baking cookies—simple activities that build and strengthen relationships as well as create meaningful memories.

5. Encourage your kid's efforts. As parents, it is all too easy to focus on misbehaviors. But it is equally important to also pay attention and recognition for your child's positive behavior. Always offer words of encouragement when your child treats other people kindly or perform a small act of kindness. In short, also catch them at their best behaviors as often as possible.

6. Promote responsibility. Offer your kids small opportunities to take care of their belongings or a family property. Most toddlers find joy in helping out adults. Of course, it's also a perfect excuse to spend more time with your child.

7. Love unconditionally. Never miss a chance of telling and showing your child how much you love them. Instilling discipline doesn't mean you need to play the bad guy. Let them know that you expect them to respect your rules but you also love them unconditionally.

These guidelines for positive parenting are not easy to adhere to, especially for parents who were not raised in the similar environment. However, by instilling positive traits and making every possible effort to be a positive parent, you create a wonderful and lasting impact and influence on your child's life, which will help them in forging relationships with other people in the future.

Guide to Surviving the Toddler Years

A lot of parents are bewildered by their toddler's behavior, especially when the child's development does not meet their set expectations. All too often we hear the same lines: **"I did everything right."** or **"I breastfed her and followed all doctor's advice."** As soon as the child turns two, parents are at a loss on how to best deal with the mood swings and the recalcitrant personality of their child.

All issues on eating, potty training, tantrums, and other developmental concerns are indeed perplexing. As most parents are already aware of, toddlers are highly unpredictable in social situations. At one time they can be extremely docile and screaming the next minute. So how does one tackle and survive these tough social scenes? Here are some great ideas to help you out:

Preparing for an Event

Most times, when it comes to dealing with toddlers, distraction is key. When going out on a social gathering, be sure to carry a full arsenal of toys, preferably those that your child do not use often. You can prepare a special tiny backpack filled with portable toys for your child to wear to make them feel responsible and important.

Empowering your Child with Responsibility

Give your child small, achievable tasks from time to time. One great example is training them to put away one toy before they can choose another one. Sometimes, it can be a bit messy and you will often find yourself doing most of the work.

However, the best way to teach a child is through consistency in setting examples.

Have your child help you with small household chores, but in such a way that they do not feel coerced or force to do so.

Try to Say Yes Most of the Time

Toddlers can be quite demanding. They cry and whine in frustration when their demands and needs are not met. A toddler's tolerance to "things not going his way" has a lot to do with how he perceives things and people going against his needs.

As parents, it is important to try and say "yes" to these needs as often as possible. When it is not possible, then you can still say "yes" and acknowledge their feelings. By respecting and meeting their needs, you will be able raise happy and cooperative child.

Most of our no's can turn to yes's quite easily. For example, a child wants to paint the wall. As much as possible, you want to accommodate their creativity, but not to the expense of ruining your wall.

A good approach is to acknowledge his want to paint the wall, and present a big sheet of paper he can paint on. Playing with a phone is a complete no-no for most parents. This can curb their need to discover things on their own. What you can do is allow them to play with the phone by unplugging it.

As long as it's safe, painless and easy to clean, parents can constantly try to be leaders in providing tools and at the same time removing obstacles. This will help children feel worthy and allows you as a parent to gain their trust on your guidance and leadership.

Most of the difficulties in toddler parenting have a lot to do with deprivations, bribes, threats, scolding and other attempts to control the child. By setting a solid example, they can grow into communicative and responsible adults at their own pace.

Chapter 7: Lesson On Raising Healthy Kids

One of the secrets to raising children who are happy, smart, and emotionally strong is to keep close watch on their health and ensure that they are fit. What your kids eat, how much sleep they get, whether or not they exercise – these will affect all aspects of their development. Even if a child has been determined to be intelligent from the get-go, if he is not healthy, there's a huge chance that he won't do as well as he could in school. Similarly, ailments and even something that seems so benign as lack of sleep can drastically affect the emotional disposition of a child. To know more about this particular secret, go through the succeeding paragraphs in this chapter.

Diet

Teaching your children healthy eating is one of the most important things you should do to be able to raise them healthily. When they're at school age, you no longer have full control over what they eat, so it's essential that they are aware which food items are good for them. It is also crucial to teach them about portion control so that they won't suffer from the negative effects that may be brought about by obesity, which is a big problem in the country.

Here are several things you can do to promote healthy eating to your children:

Eat together. If possible, have breakfast and dinner together. This will not only enhance the appetite of your kids but also force them to eat healthily (just make sure that the food served is nutritious). Sit-down meals also encourage conversation, thus making it easier for you to be updated with what is happening to your kids.

Discourage eating out often. Restaurant food is almost always calorie-laden, and brimming with salt and sugar. It is far better to eat at home, with meals that you prepared yourself. At least, you have control over what you put in the food that you and your children will eat.

Prepare healthy snacks and make these available at home. Unhealthy snacking is one of the main reasons children fail to meet the Recommended Dietary Allowance or RDA of various nutritional elements for their age, which is important in keeping or making them healthy. To address this issue, always have healthy snacks available at home so that your kids won't turn to empty-calorie items such as chips and soda when they feel like snacking.

Get the kids involved in meal preparation. Children love doing grown-up activities. As such, take this opportunity to get them involved in shopping for groceries and preparing meals, and in the process, teach them about eating healthy. Kids will get a kick out of being able to choose which healthy items will go into their lunch box, and help you prepare dishes that everyone in the family will eat.

Physical Activity

Why is physical activity important? Exercise, sports, and other physically demanding activities have been proven to have a positive effect on life expectancy because they promote good health. To elaborate, physical activity can help with weight control, blood pressure reduction, and the increase of "good" cholesterol or HDL in the body. It is likewise instrumental in the reduction of risk of several medical conditions and diseases, which include the following: diabetes, cardiovascular disease, and some forms of cancer.

Aside from the points above, physical activity can also have a positive effect on the psychological and emotional health of children. Studies have shown that kids involved in sports tend to be more outgoing, have higher self-esteem, and are more confident. Consequently, they become happier compared to those who suffer from low self-esteem or have a negative self-image.

Given the benefits of physical activity, it is evident that parents should encourage their kids to exercise, engage in sports, and/or do chores that require them to move. Although there's PE in school, you should still urge them to get moving when they are at home. Experts recommend that children 2 years of age and older should get at least an hour of physical activity every day. How can you do this? First and foremost, set an example. If you are a couch potato, your children won't be as motivated to engage in physical activities, so it's important that you make an effort to be active. Try to take them jogging with you during your free time, or encourage them to exercise with you. You can also play with them – this will likely elicit a more enthusiastic response from your kids. Another thing you can do to promote physical activity to your kids is to lessen their sedentary time. You can do this by enforcing a TV-watching and gaming schedule, and by encouraging them to lay off on using their phones all the time when they are at home by giving them chores to do.

No matter what methods you use to encourage your children to become physically active, it is important that you make sure that you inject fun into their activities whenever possible. You can do this by letting them engage in sports that interest them, or by having a reward system in place when they do household chores. Most importantly, support them in their endeavors.

Sleep

Sleep is defined in the online Merriam-Webster Dictionary as a period of suspended consciousness wherein the body works to restore itself. It likewise aids in development, that's why it's crucial that children get enough of it. Insufficient sleep can have a number of negative consequences. As with adults, it can affect your kids' disposition: they are likely to be irritable during the day. Other than this, lack of sleep can also lead to poorer focus and memory, and a delay in motor response. Health problems can also ensue if kids don't meet the number of hours of sleep for their age.

It is important that you are aware of how much sleep your children need so that you can make sure that they are having enough and make changes if they are not able to meet the recommended number of hours of sleep every day/night. Basically, the older your children get, the less sleep they require, and the need for daytime naps gradually diminishes. To illustrate this, take a look at the following points:

Infancy: During infancy, a total of 14 to 16 hours of sleep is recommended, with around 5 hours spent in daytime naps.

Toddler years: Between the age of 18 months and 3 years, children should have 12 to 13 hours' worth of sleep. Naps during the day at this time only range from 1 to 3 hours.

School-age years: From 4 to 9 years old, the recommended amount of sleep is 10-11 hours at night. During this period children may not take naps during the day altogether.

Pre-teen and teen years: When children reach 10 years of age, a minimum of 9 hours of sleep is enough to revitalize them. This can further go down to 8 hours when they are between 15 and 18 years old.

Chapter 8: Man Or Woman: Who Is A Better Parent?

Many reasons are adduced to successful parenting. When we consider this recurring theme in the family, many people are of the opinion that women are the ones who do, if not all, but most of the work of upbringing of children. Many in some quarters are not even convinced that a father or husband living under the same roof has much to offer, in terms of parental guidance of the kids.

Can we say it is true that men or fathers do not play a significant role? I think we may pardon those with that wrongful mindset. Because my own personal and direct involvement with my boys run contrary to that myth. I partly nurtured my two young boys from cradle to young men spanning a period of twenty-five unbroken years! There are abound many examples where a father with adequate presence of mind, set out with the wife to jointly nurture the progress of their children, especially boys that need a male figure. Could the myth stem from the fact that women are the first custodian of babies from the womb? Of course women are to be saluted for this huge risk, nature has bestowed upon them.But what happens after delivery? Beyond delivery, there is more to nurturing kids.

A man may not know how it feels carrying a growing fetus or multiple ones in a human body, till the painful process of natural delivery. A big applause to women for this feat, again. I respect and personally empathize with them in this wise.

We men can only imagine their pains - of almost a year's duration - a woman goes through.

Of course, a reasonable and a loving husband ought to dote on his wife and the unborn.

Dads Can Be Under Stress Too
There are many instances where some dedicated husbands, equally go through the stressful period of watching over their pregnant wife and the unborn child. The mental stress is always there for him and the wife. Even for the so-called absentee fathers, who genuinely care, they equally connect in mind, with the family, wherever they are.

I have heard of a man who temporarily lost his bearing on getting the news about the wife's unexpected laboring. He was at work. He wanted to rush home or to the hospital. He couldn't locate his car keys which was right in the bunch of keys he was holding. It was a colleague watching him in his frenzy that took the key from him and eventually drove him, straight to the hospital to be with the laboring mother-to-be.

Now, when a wife puts to bed, for some very nuclear families, some men have to do most of the domestic chores. This will include basic cooking, even if the food gets burnt while the hilarious laughter of the wife is heard at the background, as she breast-feeds or attend to the baby. There will also be the cleaning of the house, washing both the soiled clothing of the wife and baby on the first day at the hospital.

I was about 27years old when my first child - a son- was born. The rumpled and soiled clothes of my wife were dropped into my hands, that delivery morning. What a novel experience? I had to take them home to wash myself. I wasn't expecting this though. My two sons today are between twenty four years and twenty eight years as I write this. Till today, I have not really told them about this shocking experience of the past. Maybe their own situation would be different, when they eventually settle down one day. And this is what they must mentally prepare for, when they find themselves in the fortuitous journey of marriage. It's tough for both men and women, starting a family.

Chapter 9: Alarm Bells

How Could I Have Not Known?

As the mother of a troubled teen, and many years as a counselor of teens with mental and social disorders – including drug addictions – I can affirm that there are real and varied, "warning signs" that your teen may be having problems. However, for the most part such "signs" are so blooming subtle that the average parent is rarely prepared to recognize or acknowledge it as anything more than a passing phase.

I remember being highly insulted when my best friend suggested, in no uncertain terms, that my son had, "problems". To me that was absurd. Of course, hindsight is 20/20 and now, 23 years later, I clearly realize that it was true. He had problems that would plague him for decades to come.

How Could I have Not Known?

I am writing this booklet in hopes of keeping other unsuspecting parents of teens from becoming blind-sided the way I was. I want to provide a basis from which parents can make assessments of their teenager.

Not to alarm parents, but distinguishing between the attention seeking teen, who is just misbehaving to get a rise out of their parents, and one who may be starting to exhibit signs of a more serious nature could mean the difference in life and death.

The purpose of this book is not to try and turn parents into detectives, but to remind parents of how important it is that they not blow off signals that their child may be sending them. Parents, as a rule prefer to believe the best in their children. For many parents, myself included, to admit something is not quite right with their teenager, somehow meant failure as a parent.

Since your teen is the main concern here time is of the essence, so I urge parents to quickly get past the denial, anger and guilt phase. It's absolutely imperative that parents move their focus toward the more productive phase of resolution by identifying the problem and concentrating on the solution.

Is There A Problem?

All people have problems to overcome regardless of our stage of development; therefore, the question asked thus far is a rather obtrusive point.

Consequently, the question should be more logically stated as – is there a problem that puts my child at a greater risk for experiencing a life altering roadblock on their path to adulthood?

A fundamental task of responsible parenting is that of keeping yourself alert to potential dangers that can cause your youngster harm.

Hence, you have no reason to bow to the pressure - your teen or anyone else may try to impose upon you for simply asking pointed questions, and spending time talking with your teen about the serious issues of life.

Extremes

An obvious thing that is a tale tell sign of impending problems - regardless of age - is extremes. Whether it's an 18-month-old baby that can't sit up by him self, or a 40-year-old father who prefers to be at work all the time, an extreme is a signal that is worthy of attention.

If you notice that your teenager is shutting himself off from the outside world and just staying in his room unless required to be somewhere else, then that is an extreme that you may want to make note of. Another example is if his grades make a drastic change for the worse, or he starts having friends he doesn't want around his family, money is mysteriously disappearing from your change jar, and/or he no longer has an interest in the extracurricular activities he has always loved, then you may have warning signs of "extremes" worthy of attention.

Alone, most of these extremes may not be worrisome, but once extremes become chained together and a pattern has formed, a parent needs to take notice.

We recently noticed our 8-year-old grandson was taking matches from our kitchen. Upon being questioned he adamantly denied the obvious, so after giving him the fire is dangerous speech our next step is to be a little more aware of his whereabouts and actions. We don't really expect he's going to set the house on fire, but we know to be on our guard – for his sake as well as our own.

Chapter 10: Talking To Your Child So They Will Really 'Listen'

It's very easy to tell our children what to do; we do it all the time, day in and day out, don't we? But there's a difference between merely 'telling' our children what to do and doing it in a way so that they really 'listen' to what we have to say to them. Here's how we can ensure that when we speak to them, they really stand up and take 'notice' of what we have said.

Make sure you 'connect' to your child.

The best possible way you can strike that connection is to maintain a sense of eye contact. You will find that when you do, your child will take you more seriously rather than if you merely open the door to their room and mumble something before going out.

Get to the point.

A lot of times we tend to talk too much to our children and this might really end up confusing them and ensuring the message does not come across as intended. If you need to tell your child that he or she needs to clean their room, tell them so in one single sentence. Rambling about the way things are is not going to solve any purpose at all.

Make a delightful offer they simply cannot refuse.

This works especially well in the case of younger kids. You can tell them to get dressed so they can go outside and play if you are finding it hard to get them to wear their clothes after a bath. Whenever you 'offer' something to your child you will find that it removes them from their position of 'power' and helps them see things in a different light.

Use words like 'I want' instead of 'You have to'.

If you want your child to get on with doing their homework and quit playing that Play

Station of theirs, you might say something to them like 'I want you to do your homework now', instead of 'You have to do your homework now.' This will work far more effectively than you would have imagined merely because you are not in the process of ordering your children around, something that will not work that well.

Give them alternatives that are most pleasing.

You might not want your child to go alone to the park and you might wish to offer them an alternative for the same; you could tell them that they could go with several friends or offer to take them to an inside park, which is far safer than going alone. Simply telling them they can't do something is not quite enough; you have to make sure you provide them with a good alternative so they can settle for the same.

Give them time to settle down.

If your child is an emotional mess, you will find it rather difficult to get them to calm down and listen to you with effect. That is why it would be most prudent in a situation like this, to allow him or her the invaluable time to settle down. You could merely ask them to go to their room for a few moments until they have calmed down; then when they listen to you, they will be far more attentive to what you are trying to tell them.

If the discussion is closed, make sure they understand the same.

There will be times when you are rigid in your stance about certain things and even though you might have tried your best to explain things to your child in the most reasonable manner, they simply might not seem to get it at all. That is when you have to be firm and say you are sorry but you are not changing your mind. Putting your foot down in this manner will ensure you drive your point across solidly and that your child has no choice but to comply with your wishes.

Have good manners.

True, this is something most parents would want their children to have but you really need to understand that when you possess the same, the results can be extremely beneficial. You have seen how easily you comply to your child's wishes when they say things like 'Please', right? Well, it would certainly behoove you to have good manners as well when you ask your children something. Saying something like 'Please' can go a long way in getting your kids to listen to you.

Chapter 11: Challenge 2 – Emotional Adjustments

Emotional adjustments come in various forms from fear to worry. You will feel frustration, depression, and jealousy at times, as you raise your child. Going through emotional changes is natural because you have a new person to think about. Remember when you started dating, you had someone new, you had hopes, and dreams, and eventually that led you to a partner you felt you could spend your life with. You gained a partner, but you also had to adjust to living with someone, their habits, and things you might not have liked about the person or their habits.

With a baby, you are going to feel different emotions. Jealousy is an emotion you might not expect right away, but it is a common emotion that one or both parents feel. The other emotions seem more likely and more reasonable, and each will be discussed in detail.

Jealousy

Jealousy occurs when attention is divided. Perhaps one parent is paying all their waking moments' attention to the new baby. Suddenly, the other parent is feeling neglected, jealous because the baby is getting all of the attention. Jealousy can also arise when one parent is working out of the house and the other person is home all the time. The parent that is home might feel jealousy because the working parent is able to speak with adults, go out of the house without the baby along, and in general "spread their wings" a little.

It is natural to feel jealousy when a change in your life occurs based on another human being getting more attention.

Do not hide the feelings.

Accept them, instead.

If you can own your feelings, understand why they are happening, and accept that they are natural, then the jealous feelings will begin to lessen.

Worry

Two main worries plague parents: their children's health and money. Money worries begin when parents' start to realize how much it takes to raise a child. The expense of diapers, food, baby items, and as children grow older things become more expensive. Older children, such as three and up begin to like going places like zoos, museums, playgrounds, and out to eat. Parents want to provide all they can, including fun places. There are worries about saving up for school, medical needs, and much more.

A child's health is the main worry. Parents worry their children may get hurt doing something like climbing rocks, falling down, and there are always worries about disease harming a child.

There are a few ways to lessen the worries:

Don't borrow trouble—unless it has happened, don't begin worrying about it.

Child proof your home, within reason. Removing the dangers will ensure a safer child.

Make rules your child can follow as they get older, such as no climbing on the rocks unless a parent is present.

Live within your financial means. Spending money doesn't mean your children will love you any more than they already do.

Your children are going to remember the time you spent with them more than they will remember where you took them or what you bought for them. A toy can be forgotten in an hour, a hike, seeing a moose will last a lifetime. Yes, it would be great if every child got to see Disney World or Land, Hawaii, and any number of other places, but is the expense of the trip worth feeling tired, worried, and angry? No, love is everything.

Fear

Fears are like worries, just more potent. You can fear your child catching a deadly disease, dying in their crib, or being molested by a stranger. But, teaching your child to fear these things is much worse. Around your children, you need to control your fear, learn to use your fear, and not let your children see it. Your children have enough to fear, such as monsters, ghosts, wild animals, and strangers, without you being overly cautious.

Frustration

Frustration often comes about in parenting, particularly, as your children begin to test you. The words "why, how, no," and many others will be vexing. Showing your frustration all the time is never good. Your children will pick up on these emotions and feel confused. As a parent, you have to be able to use patience, whenever possible.

Even the most impatient people can learn to hide their anger and frustration. The best method is to close your eyes and take a deep breath, before starting to talk again. Some parents need to walk out of the room, stating they will be back, and calm down out of sight.

When you are frustrated with your partner, walk away or say something like, "I think we both need to stop talking and calm down before continuing, so it doesn't affect anyone else in the room."

Your children can always notice when something is amiss. They can also start adopting your behavior because they think it is acceptable.

One of the hardest challenges about children is their ability to emulate bad behavior. The irony of the situation is they can look at examples all day of bad behavior, point it out, and be unable to stop their own similar response. This can also add to your frustration.

For example, coming back from a picnic two girls in class were not listening to their teacher. The teacher called them, as did another little girl because she was trying to help the teacher. She said to a relative, "those girls never listen." Yet, at home this little girl tends to whine before asking for help, ignores a request to do something from the parent and relative, and has more than once forgotten socks or her backpack. Yet, in other children, she could recognize that they do not pay attention or listen.

When the relation of the two girls' actions is pointed out to this young girl, she gets shy or tries to make excuses for why things are different for her.

By teaching a lesson, it helps the child see their behavior. By using a comparison of behavior they notice in others, it also helps solidify the lesson. But the one thing the adult cannot do, is show the frustration they feel at repeating the lesson.

Children listen to positive words more than they listen to negative words. Becoming more positive in how you speak, can also lessen your frustrations.

Depression

For some individuals, depression is the hardest emotion to work through. Depression can be caused by many things from hormone imbalances and genetics to situational depression. Mothers, can experience post partem depression, as a result of hormonal changes. For most women in their 30s, their hormones change, they may experience rapid onset of various emotions that are hard to control, and feel more depressed around their menstrual cycle. There are options for treating this type of depression, such as St. John's Wort (with proper approval from your physician).

Depression that is situational, such as a deep feeling of loss, due to your lifestyle changes or general unhappiness, is harder to combat. Yes, there are mood correcting medications, but it is better if you can try to deal with depression without them.

Here are a couple of suggestions:

Take time for yourself.

Remember at least one good quality about yourself, on a daily basis.

Have your spouse help remind you of why they love you.

Speak with a therapist or parent support group.

There is nothing wrong with getting help from others. Do not feel like you would be putting your emotions or problems on another; especially, if they are a professional or a support group. These groups and professionals exist because help is needed.

Happiness

It can be a challenge to show or feel happy. All the negative emotions build and build, and we, as humans, tend to focus on these more negative feelings than the positives. However, reminding yourself, every day about the good things in life can bring happiness back into life.

Even if you are not feeling particularly happy, you still need to appear happy in front of your children. It is a matter of teaching your brain how to find the happiness in life, in front of your children.

Often your children can do something that will make you happy or laugh. It might be something they said that is amusing. Hold onto these memories. Use these memories on a day when things are not looking particularly good.

Love

Your children need to hear that you love them. Younger children definitely need to hear that you care about them. You can show this love through your actions and emotions. For those who do not find it easy to give hugs or say "I love you," you will need to work on it. You not only need to tell it to your children, but say it to your partner. Showing your children that you can say it to your partner will help.

It creates a loving bond between everyone in the household, so that the children realize you do love each other and do not have anything to doubt.

Chapter 12: Importance Of Child Development

For one thing, abilities are not fixed at a early age, and this happens to be the misconception that has been ruling popular belief in and around society. There is a large body of research that points to the fact that children go through a whole range of learning and develop their abilities at a very early age.

Secondly, cognitive skills are also not inherent in any child, and this is why early child development is so important to parents who want to ensure that their children are getting the best.

Thirdly, society seems to be fixated with the whole academic smarts and often force their children into aiming for high scores. Proper child development is not about high scores, but moving away from the bias of numbers and targets, and this is why we need to look at holistic development.

Another reason why you should be looking at this is that learning in any child actually begins in infancy, and most people do not realize that the moment the child is born, they start learning from their sensory perceptions and their experiential subconscious associations.

Also, the 5th point looks at the fundamentals of learning at an early age. And it reveals that when a child is engaged in early learning, the quality of the education and the learning that happens within the mind of the child has so much more quality that when it was if learning begins at a much later age.

We have to realise that the whole policy of education and learning when it comes to children is fundamentally flawed and you cannot rely upon on late stage education or any formed form of governed and mass tuned education to really develop your child.

Also, the interaction between a child and his guardians is the most basic, fundamental way that a child can learn the most effectively, and with this, early childhood development is really very important.

Since abandoning speculation in any one of these regions decreases the importance of speculation in other areas, investments to progress pre- and post-conception corporeal situation of the impending mother are an essential contribution to ECD.

Thus, preservation of all kinds to get improved parenting throughout this epoch is fundamental. This support includes expansion of parenting skills, communal help, company and administration support to augment the amount of instance parents can expend with their children and, in some cases, straight earnings support. The next three areas delve into the development progress of a child and how the time within the first 2 - 3 years of a child is the most crucial.

This is where there is plenty of association and subconscious, experiential learning that needs to be controlled and reigned in. The child needs guidance to disallow things like phobias and developmental hiccups form developing and spreading on to adulthood.

These are the ten reasons why early child development is really so important and if you are interested in the future of your child, you need to pay attention to them.

Child development is important. If your child is not developing correctly, you would recognise it by the delay in a particular behaviour that should have already been noticed. When a child has a problem in development, you need to contact your doctor immediately upon noticing it so you and your doctor can determine how to best handle the situation.

Child development milestones are certain periods in a child's life where they should already have the ability to do something. For example, walking and talking should be achieved by the age of two.

If not, then your doctor may want to do something to encourage your child to reach the child development milestone. Your doctor and other health care professionals will use these milestones to make sure that a child is developing correctly.

As a child develops, parents tend to document each and every child development milestone. Parents tend to reflect back on these milestones when they have more children so they can compare. However, everychild cannot compare to another in child development. It's important to count each child as an individual and not as a duplicate.

When a child is going through different milestones, they will work very hard to try and master the skill. For example, when learning how to walk, a child will pull up holding on to furniture, tables, and anything they can get a grip on to pull up.

When they let go, they will usually lose their footing and fall back down. It is how they learn and master the skill of walking. Soon the child will know what works and put one foot in front of the other to begin walking and succeed at reaching their child development milestone.

When a child doesn't seem to be reaching a particular developmental milestone the parent may become worried and make appointment to see the doctor. As a parent you are worried but it's also important to give your child the right amount of time to reach their milestone. Some children are more delayed than others.

The doctor will talk over the options with the parent and decide what route would be best to take. Some doctors will choose to wait until a later date to see if that child reaches the milestone at that time. If not, then other measures may be taken such as tests and a referral to specialists who can further determine if there is a reason why the child is not developing on schedule.

If you notice that your child is not reaching a child development milestone, as they should, then speak to your doctor to find out what you can do as a parent. You are your child's advocate; if you feel something is wrong, make someone listen.

If you can't get answers from one doctor or health care professional, find another doctor that could help or at least give you a second opinion to verify what the first doctor recommends.

Chapter 13: Be Firm With Affection

Kids need friendship, with firmness, direction and affection from their parents. This is not so easy to do, as we have been explaining. When your kid comes home and asks if he/she can have a tattoo, an overly popular fashion accessory, or tells you that he/she is just going to watch a movie with their friends, the last thing on their minds is the rating of the movie and you may have to set parameters. That's your job. When you have to say "no," without alienating them for the rest of their lives, it's like walking in a minefield.

Above all else, you have to give them a direction in life. You can't waver in your decisions. Stay firm but do it with affection. Kids may not understand when the hammer comes down and the decision goes against them. Then, when they grow up, they will understand and appreciate that you cared enough to impose your own rules for their safety because you cared. The worst mistake you can make is to show exactly the opposite of affection and firm by being harsh and intimidating to them. In a similar way, you should never show your kids that you give them full freedom just for the sake of peace. It may grant you some points with them in the short term, but in the long run they will become undisciplined, confused, frustrated and blame you as the source of their problems.

Another mistake is to get upset and emotional about parenthood. Kids do get emotional. They throw tantrums, they will slam doors and lock themselves up in their rooms. You shouldn't act in a way that is inappropriate for an adult. If you do, then feelings of guilt and remorse will set in, which will lead you to making bad decisions. Don't ever lose your temper and don't take their outbursts of emotion as personal. Kids can say hurtful words when they are opposed and contradicted, but that does not mean they stopped respecting you and loving you, it's all part of their own emotional game. Don't play the same game. You are an adult and should lead by example.

It is in circumstances such as this that I usually play the god cop and bad cop scenario with them. If I need to set limits and stand by our own rules, for their own good, they get upset with me. If ever I really need to raise my voice, send them to their rooms or turn my back, once they have crossed the line, my husband always stays on the sidelines and will be the one to go after our children to have a talk with them. He will let them cool down and then explain why I got mad, and the reasons why I had to put my foot down. When it is the other way around, I get to play good cop. We work as a team and that's vital to parenthood. Parents should never work one against the other. The message from each parent should be the same, even though voiced through the good cop/bad cop scenario.

Be aware of all of their relationships. You don't need to act like a helicopter-parent, always hovering over them and watching what they do, but it is important to know who their friends are and where they spend their time. Again, you don't need to be part of their friend circle, you don't need to act cool and pretend that you know everything about your children's sub-culture. Just ask them, show interest and drive them to where they want to meet their friends, keeping an eye on their spending and how they manage their time. And, never let them lose interest in their education and school achievements.

Organize and promote family activities, with your whole family. Invite your own parents, your own brothers and sisters. Your kids love to spend time with their cousins and it reinforces family values. Prepare a nice dinner for everyone, or just order some pizzas for a Saturday night session of family games. Being around their family will allow your children to understand you better, to see that your discipline and rules have a meaning and that they are part of something larger and bigger than life. Bringing them up in such an environment, allowing them to see their role in your family's history, will provide a larger horizon for their lives and bring forward stronger friendship connections with them.

You can be a friend, while also imposing authority, if you study and work with them. They will appreciate the company and help. Teach them the importance of their studies by showing them how it can affect their future. Share with them a retrospective view of your own struggles in school and teach them how you were able to overcome them. You will be just like a friend for them, studying together and dreaming about the future, together. Above all else, you also have to be diligent, honest, punctual and dutiful. Their role model will set the tone for their lives.

Raise your kids according to your fundamental character values: be truthful, brave, honest, respectful, clean, humble, organized and willing to serve others who need help. Respect your commitments towards them, and they will learn to recognize the importance of honoring their own commitments. Never leave a task without completing it because they pick up ideas from the way that you act. All of these character traits will seep into their characters and their way of life.

Chapter 14: Single Dad With A Baby:

Child-Proofing The House

You may think that your house is safe enough for your child to grow up in. But you may be in for some nasty surprises. You see once your baby starts crawling and begin learning to stand up on his own, he will also try climbing over tables, railings, chairs, and whatever else that may be in his way. Babies and toddlers have such an inquisitive character that they try to explore anything and everything within his reach. It is part of his learning process.

The problem is he doesn't know yet what can harm him. The other problem is you may not be able to keep an eye on him all the time. If you as much as turn around to answer the phone or look at who's ringing the doorbell, or get distracted by a TV commercial, the baby may already be over the railings, or has crawled inside an open cabinet and locked himself in, or inserted a pointed metal object into the electrical outlet, or swallowed or ate a harmful substance.

That's right. Any of these things can happen as you are blinking your eyes. One of your paramount responsibility as a single dad with a baby to protect is to keep him from harming himself. Your traditional role as a father is to protect the family at all times and that includes making sure that as your baby gets old enough to start exploring his surroundings, you have made it safe for him.

Somehow, it isn't right to reign in his development and put boundaries to his learning. Remember, everything he is doing is part of his learning process and constantly saying no, no, no to him every time he ventures into dangerous grounds will not be understood in the same way adults would. Worst, it may instill a rebellious attitude towards you since all your precautionary warnings (the no, no, no) will be taken as stopping him from doing what he likes to do – to explore and discover his newfound place.

Get a head start and child proof your house the moment your little explorer learn to turn himself on his stomach – because the next thing he'll try to learn is to crawl. In case your child is no longer a baby but a toddler, the need to child proof the house becomes all the more imperative. Year one to year 3 is the most hazardous time of a child's life as he knows what fear is and just wants to test and discover his surroundings to test his expanding abilities to the limits.

Get started by going down on your knees and look at everything from the baby's perspective – anything from the ground up to four feet from the floor will be reachable by the child. You call this a 'crawl through' - an exercise you need to do every now and then to make sure nothing is there that can do harm to the baby. Think of what is likely to happen when the baby starts crawling all over the place and begin climbing, pushing, or pulling things.

If you don't have the faintest idea on what you should be looking for, here are some childproofing ideas that should help you get started.

Look for all the electrical outlets all over the house and cover each one with a safety cap the baby can't possibly pull out. Make sure you don't miss any. Install ground fault circuit interrupters or GFCI in all the electrical outlets in the kitchen and bathroom outlets. GFCIs automatically cuts off electricity to any appliance that is plugged to it which accidentally comes in contact with water.

Keep all the electrical appliances unplugged when not in use with their cords rolled up and secured well beyond the baby's reach. For appliances that need to be constantly plugged use specially designed electrical plugs that can't be pulled out easily by the child. There are a number of them available in hardware stores.

Consider putting safety gates at the top and the bottom of stairs but don't buy gates has pressure bars which expands as the baby can get caught in between.

Use doorknob covers on doors leading to areas hazardous to kids such as the garage and the swimming pool. Make sure though that the door knob covers are easy enough for adults to take out during emergencies but sturdy enough to discourages kids from going through.

Bolt down furniture that are likely to tip over. Tall drawers with chests must also be strapped to the wall as they may fall over if the child attempts to push, pull, or climb it.

Cover tables, chairs, and other furniture with sharp edges and pointed corners with soft or cushioned bumpers. Your baby won't get hurt if he accidentally loses his balance and hit any of them.

Put a lock on toilet lids. Kids are top heavy and if they attempt to climb the toilet bowl they are likely to fall inside it and drown.

Install locks or special latches on drawers and cabinets that are low enough for the baby to reach and open. Keep the doors of the refrigerator, freezer, dishwasher, oven, and dryers locked. There are special locks for kitchen appliances you can buy at your favorite hardware stores.

Bolt your stove to the wall. If a child manages to open the oven door, he is likely to stand on top of it which could topple the entire stove possibly pinning the child under it.

Make sure the stove knobs are properly covered. It's a matter of time before your child will be able to reach it and turn the gas on. Remember, kids almost always copy what the elders around them are doing. When he is small and can't still reach the knobs, the curiosity may linger in his mind and when he is finally able to reach the knobs he may just turn on the gas.

Don't place furniture near windows. Babies may use them to climb to the window sills. Even if your windows are screened, there is still that possibility the baby may fall through the window if the screen is not sturdy enough to keep the child inside.

Keep all your detergent, cleaning agents, and other household chemicals in a locked cabinet unreachable even by toddlers.

You should also keep all medicines including the baby's medicines in a medicine cabinet which is out of kids' reach.

Make it appoint to cover the bathtub spout when you give the baby a bath in the tub. The kid won't get hurt or burn himself if he accidentally touch or hit it.

If you have a swimming pool, make sure you always keep it covered. There's no telling when your kid will slip out of your sights and go to the pool area.

Don't put any breakable items particularly those made of glass in the way of your kids. Keep them away someplace safe and out of their reach.

Never leave water in the bathtub, buckets or any large container that can be reached by the kid. Kids can drown in them.

Chapter 15: The Arrival: Game In Session

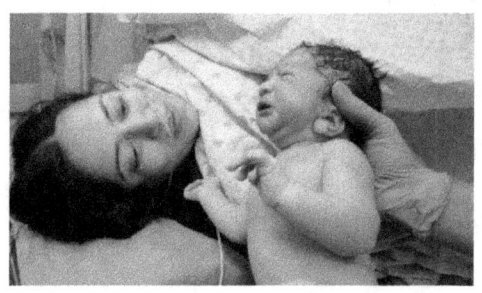

The Kickoff (aka Labor and Delivery)

Start the water and boil the car. It's game time! Suddenly, everything is in slow motion, like a dream. You know, the kind where you are running for a touchdown... the wrong way... in your underwear.

False vs. Real Labor

Sometimes there's what you might call a scrimmage. It's also called false labor. While false labor can get you all warmed up for the game, it can also leave you emotionally drained, especially if it happens over and over (and sometimes it does).

Braxton Hicks

Braxton Hicks are different from actual false labor. They are contractions that happen during pregnancy, mostly during the last trimester. The contractions cause the abdomen to tighten and can last anywhere from a few seconds to a few minutes in duration, but they are irregular, painless and end up going away.

The Difference is?

The main difference between Braxton Hicks and false labor is that false labor is closer to actual labor. Although it is usually sporadic with irregular timing, it can be uncomfortable and sometimes even classified as painful where Braxton Hicks are not painful. Like Braxton Hicks contractions, false labor goes away.

The Real Deal

True labor doesn't go away. The pains become noticeably stronger and begin to last longer. Contractions will begin to take on a pattern with regular intervals and will come closer and closer together.

When the contractions are coming fairly regularly, go ahead and call the doctor. The doctor will most likely want the two of you to go to the hospital when the contractions are coming about every five minutes and are lasting for around one minute. The way to time them is from the beginning of one until the start of the next.

If you live in a remote area, the pregnancy is high risk, the weather is bad or there is any other unusual factor, you will be given other instructions or will make your own call. Babies have been born in route to the hospital so never hesitate to call or just head that way unless you want to deliver the baby yourself.

When the time comes, you will probably panic. Don't worry. She'll calm you down.

The main thing you need to remember is the directions to the hospital. Oh, and to have enough gas in the car. Don't forget that!

Once you are safely at the hospital and it's confirmed your wife will be admitted, your baby will arrive in due time. Then you can make phone calls and get ready to coach. Your wife will need you more than ever so bring your best game.

Labor and Delivery Vocabulary List

Before going any further, it's helpful to get familiar with some words you will hear during labor and delivery. Here's the list:

Labor	The process of getting your baby from point A to point B.
Early Labor	When your wife first begins contractions. Usually during this time, the doctor is called and preparations get underway to get to the hospital.

Active Labor	Things begin to heat up. If you are not yet at the hospital, you'll want to get there. If you are there, you will begin to get a glimpse at what is yet to come. Your wife is getting pretty uncomfortable during contractions.
Advanced Labor	Pain! Every woman experiences labor differently but few (if any) have ever said it was painless. Expect to be the man you can be, coaching her through contractions with just a breather in between them.
Effaced	The thinning of the cervix in preparation of the birth.
Dilation	The opening of the cervix in preparation of the birth. Doctors like to wait until the

	dilation is at a 10 before your wife pushes but there are exceptions.
Neonatal	Things that have to do with a newborn infant.
Breech	When the baby's feet are at the cervix rather than her head. Thus, the expression "feet first". This is not an ideal position and if the baby doesn't reposition, a Caesarian Section may be in order or a forceps delivery.
Bite	What your wife will probably do to your during hard labor.
Forceps	A tool used to assist in delivery if needed.
Caesarian Section	Surgically delivering the baby. Also known as C-section.
Umbilical	The lifeline between your

Cord	baby and his mother that will be cut once he is born. You may be asked if you want to do the honors. If so...the answer is "yes" or you will never live it down.
Prep	What the nurses will do to your wife to get ready for the birth such as the shaving of pubic hairs and perhaps and enema.
Push	The action taken by the baby's mamma at the end of labor to get the baby out. The nature of labor is that she will enter a pushing stage and will have the natural, overwhelming urge to push.
Crowned	When the baby's head is ready to come out.
Perfect	Your baby

Timing is Everything

The length of labor can vary greatly. No two women are the same and no two labors of the same woman are the same. Let's go through the entire process so you will not find yourself surprised (or worse, passed out on the floor).

Once she goes into labor and gets to the hospital, she will be admitted, prepped and monitored. At some point during labor, her amniotic fluid sack will break or the doctor will break it. Maybe it broke before you got to the hospital. Once it's broken, labor usually proceeds rather quickly.

First time births generally take longer so be prepared to stay awhile. Don't worry about bringing things to do. Your wife will have plenty to keep you busy.

The object of the game is for the cervix (the opening into the womb where the baby has been living) to dilate. When it has reached three centimeters, she is considered to be in active labor. Doctors prefer for her to reach a full 10 centimeters before the baby is delivered.

The process in between involves contractions that will begin to get stronger and closer together. During a contraction, your wife's abdomen will get hard and it will hurt. Prior to labor, the two of you can discuss the option for pain relief and can also change your plan in mid-stream as long as the process is not too far along.

Some women experience labor pains in their abdomen and pelvic area. Some have the blunt of it in their back. Trust me, there will be no guess-work. She will let you know.

Take your bottom lip and pull it up over your head. That is a good analogy of what labor feels like. Do all that you can; give her ice chips, let her slap you around because you "got her pregnant in the first place" and encourage as well as praise her all that you can. But realize that you cannot stop the pain. It's just a natural process the two of you have to get through together.

Team "Baby"

If you have ever taken part in team building exercises particularly with sports, you know how valuable they can be. Talent wins games, but teamwork builds championships. You really never hear of a football team winning the Super Bowl that didn't play well together. The same is true for the World Series and the World Cup.

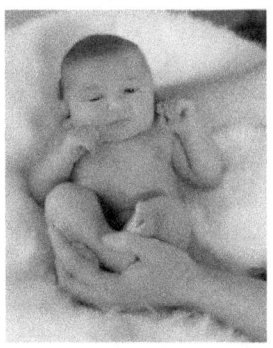

You are probably wondering how having a baby could be anything but bliss. Or, maybe you know better. Trust me, once the "babymoon" is over... it's over. There will be plenty of sleepless nights, not just for your baby, but also for you and your baby's Momma, too. Nerves will get raveled, tension will run tight. You need a back-up plan and you need to have it in place before you leave the hospital with your little one.

There are some problems you and Mommy may encounter. Let's take a look at them and explore solutions, too.

Sleep Deprivation

Newborns sleep an average of 15 to 16 hours in a twenty-four hour time period.

So why is it that her parents walk around like zombies?

Just because your little one sleeps so much certainly doesn't mean that you will. Baby's sleep is usually done in two or three hour intervals throughout the day and night. The sleep cycle of a baby is scientifically set up to thrive on her schedule, but it is exhausting for the parents because you are not hitting the deep sleep that revives, rejuvenates and heals your body.

Here are some symptoms that may occur.

Grogginess

Depression

Brain Fog

Irritability

Lethargy

Lowering of resistance to illnesses

Excessive worry

There are some measures you can take to balance the tiredness. Trade out shifts with your partner. If she is nursing, it's a little more complicated but there are still several options. She can pump her breast milk so you can give the baby a bottle instead. She can feed the little one and then go on to bed while you change and rock him or whatever needs to be done. The shift work can be determined by taking into consideration your work schedule, her work schedule if she has an outside job and also by who is holding up the best under the stress.

Being Socially Isolated

Both you and your significant other will most likely feel a little isolated after your baby is born. At first, there will be a flood of visitors but when that subsides, you will find your social life does as well. A childless couple with whom you used to associate may not invite you to do things. You will think twice before taking the baby out for visits. You and/or the baby's Mom may take family leave from work and no longer be around your co-workers. It can get lonely.

Cheer up. Some things that can remedy the shut-out feelings are:

Do the inviting yourselves.

Have a trusted friend or family member watch the baby for a short time while you take your other half to dinner.

Set aside entertaining activities while your little one sleeps, such as watching a movie together.

Take turns; let her go do something such as have lunch with a friend and you go out bowling with the guys on the next go around.

Realize that the situation is temporary. This too shall pass!

Balance

When it comes to things like deciding who is doing the most work where the baby is concerned, chances are good it will be Mom. Nothing you can say or do will change that fact. But, there are some things you can do to get a better balance. Remember, balance is not found... it's created.

If you are handy in the kitchen, cook some or all of the meals. Otherwise, order take-out at least once a week.

Run her bath water and take over baby duties while she takes a nice, long bubble bath. Better yet, throw some soothing essential oils in the mix. Lavender works wonders.

Choose some baby jobs, like bathing him, and relieve her of that duty each time it needs to be done.

Take a little time off work if you can. She could use the help!

It is estimated that almost half of the marriages within the United States will end in divorce. Especially now that you have another person to consider, the chips are stacked against you, but with a little planning and a lot of effort, you can beat the odds. You have got to be a team player if you want you want to be a winner and now... it's all about Team Baby.

Mom's Body After Baby

It is rare that a woman comes out of a pregnancy unscathed. She will most likely have a few (ok... maybe a lot) of stretch marks on places like her tummy, the back of her hips, her legs, breasts and possibly her buttocks. Some women get dark patches on their face during pregnancy and those should fade after the birth, but sometimes they don't. Chances are that her breasts will grow if she is nursing, only to shrivel a bit after weaning. And guess what? She may even keep a few of the pounds she put on while pregnant.

Although a pregnancy does some not-so-great things to her body, it is a miracle the two of you have born a new life. It's a small price to pay! If you are like most men, you will love her so much more it won't even begin to matter.

And here's what you are really wondering—having sex after your wife has delivered a normal vaginal birth is recommended to be delayed until she has her first postpartum check-up at six weeks before having intercourse. Don't panic. The two of you will be quite busy and the time will fly by but otherwise, the rule usually only applies to vaginal intercourse.

Being a Great Home Team Player: The Science Behind It

As guys, be encouraged that some of the obstacles you will face as a new Dad are scientifically based. Wired posted an article in July 2014 entitled "How

Becoming a Father Changes Your Brain" that talks about a number of changes.

First, when you become a new father, the grey matter within your brain increases. One place this occurs is in the striatum, the area where reward is recognized. Another is in the hypothalamus, which controls hormones. The anterior cingulate cortex also gets activated, where emotional processing is regulated. The lateral prefrontal cortex, responsible for decision making and memory, are affected as well. Wow! No wonder you can be expected to be a mess.

That's not even mentioning the brain changes the Mom will encounter. Her hormones will be raging and hormones are not just feelings. They are emotions caused by scientific reasons. She will be more protective. She will worry. And... she will experience love like never before. It's all part of the science.

Also, she may get "the blues", otherwise known as Postpartum Depression (PPD), a condition that is not uncommon among new mothers. Forty to eighty percent of all new moms experience it. It is very real and can be very serious. If your wife is showing signs of depression that are not going away (such as excessive crying or loss of interest), please contact her physician.

When she seems depressed - even if you can't figure out why - now is the time to go above and beyond the call of duty. Make her a nice dinner without being asked. Clean up the evening meal's dishes. Do a load of laundry. You'll not only help her out, you'll lift your own spirits for having done something noble.

Armed with the knowledge that there are scientific based reasons behind the strong emotions that will fly around, you will be better equipped to deal with them just like a team taking on a really great team studies them to gain any kind of an edge, being prepared is the key.

Chapter Takeaways

False labor is irregular in nature and the contractions go away. Braxton Hicks contractions are quite common, but are not true labor.

When the time comes and labor is in progress, it is important to know what lies ahead so you can be supportive and remain upright (not passed out on the floor).

Crowning is when the baby's head is in place, ready for delivery.

Babies sleep in two to three hour intervals, which means you and your wife will get little uninterrupted sleep.

Working as a team, you and your baby's mother can make plans to get through all the hurdles together.

Chapter 17: How Do You Connect With Your Teenager?

This is probably the most important question that you have to answer, and you truly need to answer it before you try and answer any of the other questions that we're going to explore in this book. Why? Because if you aren't connected with your teenager, and your teenager doesn't know that you love them unconditionally, none of the advice that we're going to give from here forward will work.

This is because all of the advice that we're going to give is based on a foundation of trust. If your teenager doesn't trust you, and you don't trust them, it's not going to end well for either one of you. You'll try these techniques and they will become suspicious and wonder if you are trying to manipulate them or get them to do something that they don't want to do. So what can you do in order to prevent that from happening? How can you develop a relationship with your teenager that helps you to have mutual trust, which in turn will help you to talk with them in a reasonable manner when topics like these come up?

The best place to get started is by just listening to them. Even if you have multiple children, take them on "dad dates" or "mom dates," starting when they are very young. These dates are just supposed to be fun; you can take them for ice cream, or to lunch, or even just to the grocery store for some groceries. During these times, you need to let them know that they are the most important thing in the world to you, and keep the floor open so that they can talk about whatever they want or need to talk about. It may seem awkward at first, but by doing this on a regular basis (every other week, once a month even), both of you will get used to it and even start embracing the time that you have together. Establishing this habit early on will make the teenage years a bit smoother.

Another way to connect is for you to find common interests and talk about them and/or enjoy them together. For example, I know a family where their teenage daughter is very interested in "nerdy" things, like classics and Shakespeare. The mom is not interested in those things at all, and instead is interested in fitness, working out, and those sorts of things. Where could you find a bridge? They found one in British television, which they enjoy together at least once a week. Even if you feel as if you and your teen are total opposites, there is something that you can connect with. Once you find it, take advantage of it! It could be a stepping stone toward other connections.

Be involved in your teenager's life. If they are involved in a club or organization, you need to support them, even if you have no interest in the topic at hand. Sometimes, it means even more that way because your teen recognizes how genuinely interested you are in their individual interests and likes. You, as the parent, need to be their biggest cheerleader, whether you're doing that at their football game or during their school play. If they see that you are genuinely interested in what they are doing, then they will be more likely to tell you what's going on in other areas of their lives.

One of the biggest mistakes that my family made when I was growing up was that we never ate dinner together unless it was a holiday. So the only times that I ate with other people were holidays or when I was at a friend's house. Why is eating together so important? Food encourages conversation. Even if you're not used to all sitting at the table, doing so once a week can help foster relationships and make everyone in your family feel as if they belong as part of the unit. We live in a fast paced world; you don't necessarily have to make something fancy. You could bring home fast food and this would still work; the point is that you're eating together.

There are plenty of other things that you can do in order to connect with your teenager; the above suggestions are just that: suggestions. There are many other ideas out there that you can try. And keep in mind; some of these tips likely won't work for you. You need to find what works, eliminate what doesn't, and then move forward in your journey of connecting with you teen. Making that initial connection with your teenager is an excellent (and necessary) part of the process of helping them through these turbulent years.

Chapter 18: Motivating Kids On Their Choice Of Life Through Proactivity Over Reactivity

What is the essence being 'proactive' as opposed to 'reactive'? Most importantly, how can you help your kids understanding the meaning, importance and concept of proactivity? This chapter discusses proactive over reactive thinking.

Being reactive means one lacks the drive and passion to take initiative. Whenever they act, it is not because they sat down, thought and planned it out. They are merely being thrown around by the events. A reactive person tends to be a victim of circumstances and their agenda is determined by the winds of change. With each change, reactive thinkers are caught by surprise and try to 'make things right.' However, they are always several strides behind.

Proactive is quite a contrast to reactive. Proactive people graciously set the pace without being stressed. Being proactive means one is in sync with the events around them. Instead of drowning in the situation, there is an understanding of what is going on. Being proactive people, they always see the positive in every situation and work towards achieving their goals.

As a parent, it is important to understand the proactive trait is not hereditary. Unlike other qualities, it has nothing to do with genetics. Instead, this quality can be developed and cultivated. Parenting includes bringing your child up as best as you can. Teaching them to be proactive is one of the best gifts you can ever give to them.

Although "proactive" and "reactive" sound opposite and very dissimilar, they are similar in more ways than you could imagine. Matter-of-factly, being proactive is the same as being reactive. The only difference is that proactivity means reacting ahead of time. Understanding this simple explanation can drastically improve your parenting skills.

The question is; "how to teach your kids to be proactive?" The trick is to understand that the lesson lies in perspective. A proactive child is taught that life is not always smooth sailing. In fact, there are more tides than calm. Instead of being overwhelmed, they will look at the situation from a systematic approach. Knowledge of what to expect arms your children with the ability to develop consistency and develop logical explanations.

Therefore, motivating your child on their choices of life through proactivity over reactivity. It means that they will be able to anticipate the uncertainty of life. When the uncertainty hits, they will react in a calm, positive manner and come out victorious.

When kids are taught well, there will be no break from being a proactive person. Your children embody the meaning and grow with them. They can even take them to the workplace. International agencies are also applying proactive solutions to everyday challenges. An excellent example of "Reactive or Proactive", which is also a case study, is published in the MeetingsPR blog which includes a crisis communication checklist for PR and social media meetings. (See Table-1)

Therefore, the highlight is that proactivity is needed and it becomes a lifetime skill. The most important stage to teach proactivity is during teenage hood. At this stage, most parents find their kids to be volatile and ready to snap. However, it should be understood that this is the stage at which self—discovery happens. As a parent, your duty is to instill good values to your child from as little as possible. Even when they start rebelling in their teenage years, it won't be as bad as that of someone who does not have a strong background.

Table-1: Examples of Reactive and Proactive Languages are shown below:

Reactive Language	Proactive Language
Why am I being controlled?	What should we do next?
What is the trend of universities good for me?	Which university is good for me and how will I get there?
I don't have time	How shall I make time
How much money can I make if I do this?	How much money do I want to make?
Let me try that can	I will make it

do or not	happens
It is too stress for me	I will do it
I've never been very good in Math	How can I improve my Math?
I can't afford fail	I will gain experience from the failure
What is the meaning of life?	What is the meaning of giving my life?

You, as a parent, need to be as open as possible so that your children learn from you. An open policy creates a healthy environment. In a healthy environment, children easily absorb information.

Reactive people seem to be lack of information. However, when your kids are informed, they naturally become proactive. Teach your kids to ask themselves what can happen in the future. Whenever any situation eventually occurs, they are prepared for it. Even in case your kids are reluctant to be proactive, be patient to them. Take your time and understand their reactivity as a symptom that needs to be cured. Over time, they will learn, simple by observing you. Hence, it is uttermost important to practice what you teach. You must stay proactive, and your children will copy from you!

Chapter 19: Guidelines For Becoming An Effective Step Parent

The most essential errands confronting a step family is figuring out what role the step parent will play and when he or she will start assuming that role. Generally, powerful step parents build up their role bit by bit. Youngsters and natural parents alter best when they are included in the formation of this role. Step parents are best when the role they play is a characteristic one for them, using their qualities and endowments in the family.

Following are a few rules that we have gathered from listening to other step parents. Utilize this rundown as your family works out a powerful step parent role:

Begin minimally: Step parents enter the family with almost no status contrasted with the biological parent. This status evolves gradually as the child sees the step parent as somebody who can be trusted. Partner and children improve if you are receptive to the necessities of the youngsters. The best way to deal with this method early is to be around and observe the youngsters. Give the kids a chance to unwind and feel safe when you are around. Keep your motivation basic.

Timing is everything: Oppose the allurement to parent too early, regardless of what your partner says or does. Your viability as a parental figure is in direct extent to the nature of the relationship you have created with the youngster. Give yourself and your step children time. Being tolerant and permitting a role to grow gradually is one of the hardest yet most vital things a step parent will do. As a rule, the younger the kid, all the more promptly the step parent is acknowledged.

Try not to usurp the role of the biological parent: Youngsters need affirmation of their extraordinary relationship with the biological parent, whether he or she is affectionate or abusive.

Pressure to desert, to belittle, or to overlook the presence of a parent places the kid in an extreme reliability dilemma that will restrain his or her capacity to frame an association with the new step parent. You are not there to supplant the non-custodial or missing parent. Discover a role that supplements the role of the biological parent. Try not to endeavor to avoid them from imperative occasions in their kid's life.

Support the role of the biological parent: Step parents ought to discover a role that compliments the biological parent. They can turn into a neutral sounding board for their partner, for instance, somebody who listens to their disappointment about the youngsters without feedback. They can likewise give information and perception to the biological parent. A step parent will spot issues that the biological parent is not prepared to recognize or manage. In such cases, the step parent must give the parent time to travel through the issues. Driving perspectives on the biological parent or transparently contradicting them will unavoidably bring conflict.

Chapter 20: Truths About Single Parent Statistics

Being a single parent is one of the world's hardest positions anyone can be in. There are many harsh statistics regarding parents. It reflects the way our lives are being lived today. The United States alone has 14 million parents who are single raising 21.6 million children. Most of these parents are moms. Most parents are either separated or divorced.

Categories of single parents from statistics

About 83.1% of children custody is awarded to mothers with 16.9% to fathers.

Single moms who are divorced or separated account for 45% while single moms who are not married account for 34%. Widows take up 1.7% with single employed moms at 80%, fulltime working moms at 50% and part-time working moms at 30%. There are still 27% single moms living in poverty.

For single fathers, 58% of them are divorced or separated; 20% have remarried while 21% never married. Less than 1% is widowed and 90% single dads are working with 19% part-time and 72% fulltime.

Struggles of single parents

Parents encounter a lot of difficulties which they have to struggle on their own, even if they have some form of support. Parents need to juggle between work and children; house and finances; food and activities; school and tuition. There is no spouse to take half the load. There is little time for self.

These statistics show the growing population of parents. They reveal the growing problems a parent household faces in finance, education, work, raising children and self development. The statistics can also reveal the growing mental health of parents as they go through their struggles alone.

What the statistics are cautioning

There may be a growing number of delinquency issues from parent homes as the parent is usually not available to cater to the needs of the children. These statistics give insight into potential problems that can besiege the family; hence, our society may be negatively impacted.

Parents need to adjust to their role as provider and caregiver to ensure a wholesome development of themselves and their children. Time alone and time with their children are required to ensure that statistics on juvenile delinquency, child abuse, alcoholism, drug addiction and the like do not climb.

It is important to have the right support for parents and their children to avoid the negative impact of parenting. Support groups and financial aids may play a large and important role in single parents' new lifestyle but developing the right relationship between parent and child is also very essential to develop a healthy home.

Benefits of Being a Single Parent

Single parents are found in every society in the world today. This implies that there are many broken families that are formed due to one reason or another.

However, many nations are mindful of the difficulties and struggles a parent goes through and put in as many benefits to assist the parent. A parent will have at least one child to care for and that will be a long and heavy investment. You can check out if you, as a parent, qualify for the federal benefits.

Eligibility of single parent benefits

Firstly, age matters. A parent can be of any age. A parent below the age of 16 to 19, in full time studies or intending to be employed in that same age bracket is eligible to federal assistance in terms of financial aid.

There are many charitable organizations, corporations and support groups for parents that offer much more besides financial aid.

Emotional support

A parent cannot cope with all the emotions that may swell up in various caring situations; hence, a support group is crucial to maintain the mental and emotional health of a parent. Regular meet ups with such support groups prove to be a great benefit to parents who need to learn how to care for their children while juggling between jobs and family. The role of a parent is quite demanding to function as a father and mother.

You may find loads of information on techniques and ways to care for your children as a parent, but none is as effective as meeting with other parents and professional counselors who can share from live experiences.

Free school program

Parents can benefit from a federal incentive for parents where their children can get schooling benefits such as free tuition, food and study materials. This would ease the burden of parents, especially if there is more than one child in the family.

Health benefits

There are certain health benefits for parents that qualify you for free medication or medical check ups for yourself and your children if you are a parent. There may be some visits from the local child or family services department to check on your state of livelihood.

Some states include free or discounted dental treatments, glasses and vision tests or travel options.

Community benefits

There may be community care and share programs for parents where free activities are offered to parents and their children such as public library access and membership, plays and local activities. Assistance of sorts may be offered free of charge for parent families.

Various Grants for Single Parents

With the cost of living on the rise every year, it is getting more difficult for single parents to make ends meet. Hence, grants for parents are necessary. There are a few grants for parents if they meet the requirements stipulated for each grant.

Federal grants

Most governments have set aside some funds known as grants for parents for upgrading their academic qualification so that they can be more competitive in their career. With a better job, parents can provide better living conditions to their children.

In the U.S. there are two such grants for parents: the Academic Competitiveness Grant and the Pell Grant. These grants for parents are given to parents who are earning low income but want to develop themselves academically.

Single parents need to submit an application for such grants through the local welfare office in their district.

Entrepreneur Grants

Such grants for single parents especially single mothers are set up to empower parents to set up their own simple business which they can manage and reap a profit to cater to the needs of their family. This personal business set up allows parents more flexibility with their time to cater to the needs of the home and children. They are empowered to control their business as they develop independence over their financial demands.

Private sector grants

Grants for parents can also come from the private sector like big companies; these may be more possible if you as a single parent are working in such a company. Big organizations are usually open to participate in charitable deeds like giving grants to parents in an attempt to enhance their image in the public as well as to reduce their taxes.

You can write in to big organizations requesting for a consideration of grants to parents or look out for their advertisements in the dailies. You can also check out various companies' websites for such opportunities.

Grants from religious sources

There are many religious groups which offer grants for parents depending on the number of recipients and quantum of financial assistance. These are private funds distributed to needy parents on a compassionate basis according to the religious teachings of each religious group.

Grants from charitable sources

There are many charitable organizations which are specially set up to provide grants for parents to ease their financial difficulties. These charitable organizations are usually the charitable arms of big conglomerates that want to exercise corporate social responsibility or to lower their taxable income.

Scholarship Programs For Single Parents

Single parent families, that are those, which have only one person as the head of the family, are growing in numbers every year. Such families are usually the result of parental breakup and unwanted pregnancies. More than men, women are the ones who get into this difficult situation. They are not only required to feed the family but also support everyone emotionally.

Single mom families are commonly seen in areas wherein unemployment is rampant. A lot of times teenage single mothers are forced to stop their education and start earning because otherwise no one would take care of their kids. Due to unfinished schooling, such single mothers have a lower income capacity.

Several government, state, and various universities and colleges offer scholarship to single parents especially to female single parents who are determined to improve their earning potential. These colleges fund for their dorm fees, tuition fees and other related educational expenses.

One of the major reasons for offering scholarships to single parents is to pave the way for increasing income potential of single families. Most universities share the same global vision of giving hope and improving confidence of the single parents by offering scholarship programs.

Scholarship for single parents usually covers the tuition fees, books and other related educational expenses of the eligible candidates. Some source of scholarships for single parents also provided restrictions to those who want to avail the scholarships.

Any scholarship for single parent is offered to those single parent students who have at least one dependent child and who desperately need financial help. So, if the single parent gets married during the terms of the scholarship, her grant can get revoked.

Those single parent students who get specific support from their families, such as willingness to take care of kids while the parents are in school, may avail of full time class scholarships. For those single parents who cannot leave their children (such as in case of disabled or mentally challenged kids) may avail of single parent scholarships that offer part-time class load requirements.

Single parent students covered by scholarships for single parents are being trained to enhance their skills on writing, interpersonal communication and computer. Single parent students are also taught of the learning techniques for success and career exploration.

Many scholarship programs for single parents require that students pass their examination with a minimum grade. Just to give an example, a single parent may be required a passing grade of 3.0 grade-point averages while other students require a 2.5 GPA. There are other scholarships that ask for repayment too when the single parents finish their education.

Some scholarships for single parents have very strict attendance requirements. It is advised to look for scholarships that provide convenience and flexibility because all the single parents play double roles at their home.

As such, there are many courses and programs that single parent may choose from. But mostly, the scholarships are extended to the following courses: accounting course, business courses, computer courses, interior design, health services and office management. Depending on individual strengths and skills, single parents can select appropriate courses.

Single parents who have the desire to continue their education but lack the financial aid may search for scholarships for single parents online at the websites of universities and colleges or even government websites. You may also call or visit some colleges to check if they are offering scholarship for a single parent like you.

The scholarships for single parents are offered by many governments and states too. In case of state scholarships, single parents are granted the amount of tuition, books and dorm for two years until they finish their graduate program.

Single parents who decide to pursue their education must explain to their children the benefit of finishing their studies. Enlighten your children's mind that before you achieve the success both of you must sacrifice for your time will be divided between your studies, work and them.

There are scholarships for single parent students, which not only help the parents but also their children. This kind of scholarship program facilitates services for their students by taking care of the children while the parent students are in school. These kinds of scholarships are limited depending on the funds of the donors of the scholarships.

Such kind of scholarship benefits not only the single parents but also their children. The services offered for children typically aim at educating and preparing children for pre-school and public school. Children from the age of 12 months of age can avail this facility throughout their school life.

It's up to every individual single parent to understand and take advantage of scholarship programs.

Chapter 21: Take Care Of Their Health

The mental and physical health of your child are strongly interrelated and equal in their importance and significance in maintaining their health for longer periods. The childhood period is one of the most critical periods in which alterations, creations and modifications of the personality and health of the individual can be radically maintained throughout life. Having previously spoken about proper establishment of the mental health of the child, including their psychology and personality. The establishment of the physical health is never less important, and it is important to highlight that even the slightest violations and impairments can incur irreversible and massive unfavourable outcomes by the time your little one becomes no longer little.

So, what are the available methods to preserve the child's physical health and take proper care of it? There actually exist numerous methods, some of which are the most common, easiest yet most important to implement:

No underestimation of any abnormal symptom or sign manifested by your child, even if they do not complain about anything. It is noteworthy to draw your attention to the fact that a number of paediatric diseases and conditions can sometimes begin insidiously (secretly, in a hidden pattern, without any symptoms or apparent signs). Do not hesitate to refer to specialists once you notice something unusual. Trust your intuition when it insinuates to you that something is not right. Do not wait until matters become complicated. The later you take an action, the less favourable outcomes might become.

It is highly recommended to refer to special health establishments even when nothing is wrong with your child. The process of prophylaxis, or prevention, is very much advised by doctors and very much recommended to be approached as it spares a lot of sufferings and unwanted complications that may attend in case no preventive measures have been taken. Your child has the right to be checked regularly to assess their health condition, detect any problems or potential problems and take prompt and early action against them.

Pay attention to what you feed your child. Yes you can spoil them when it comes to eating, but not too much! Remember that too much fast food is never good for weight and cholesterol levels. Too much chocolates and sweets is no good for teeth and blood sugar, as well as weight. If you can accustom your child to boycott soda drinks, that would be ideal. Increase the amount of fruits, vegetables, milk, natural proteins and fibres in your child's diet. The little body is in need for these products and elements to develop healthily and properly, away from diseases that are not supposed to attend at such an early age.

Tell your child how good it feels to smile with white, clean and healthy teeth. You can show some relevant pictures to implant the stamina. Accustom your child to brush the teeth twice to thrice a day: if twice, upon waking up and before bed. Referring back to being a good role model, being witnessed by your child brushing your teeth regularly would almost certainly drive them to act similarly, rather than being dictated what to do without you being a positive illustration of it.

Do NOT neglect vaccinations! They are one of the most fundamental rights to be received by your child. They must not be delayed for long nor cancelled. Vaccinations are carried out usually at local health establishments, to which you can refer for further information about vaccinating schedules. You must realise the massive danger you would be exposing your child to if you for any reason choose to deprive them of this right. The first of these danger stands for immunodepression/immunosuppression (wherein the immune system of your child is suppressed/depressed), rendering your child vulnerable to a spectrum of illnesses of various levels of severity, some of which can be fatal.

Do NOT give any medication to your child independently of consulting a specialist. Drugs that may be of a mild effect to adults may be dangerous and toxic to children.

Chapter 22: Limits And Rules: When You Should Tell Your Child 'Yes' And 'No'

Boundaries are a framework, a guideline that shows which behavior is acceptable and which is not, and must be clear, concrete and well defined. When setting boundaries, it is important to be consistent, because that way the child will know that the boundaries cannot be negotiated at different times and places. The child must understand that the boundaries you set for them are not something that is disputable or variable.

The boundaries must be set, and within that framework, certain rules have to be made. However, that doesn't mean that those rules need to be overly strict.

It is clear that growing up within positively defined limits is the best way for a child to gradually develop life skills and learn to deal with everyday challenges, therefore those limits need to be set up in a timely manner. It is also important to make sure to establish an atmosphere of love and acceptance before, and not after, problems arises. Boundaries are, therefore, the framework, the guidelines that show which behavior is acceptable and which is not, and must be clear, concrete and well defined.

The difference between a children's wants and needs

When a child asks his parents for permission to do something, the parent needs to determine the answer based on the values and rules that they and their family hold. Certainly, before we say no to something, we need to to think carefully, so as not to constantly change the rules, but at the same time, it is necessary to keep in mind that the boundaries are not "set in stone," but that with time they need to be changed and adjusted according to developmental age of a child.

When setting boundaries, we must know how to distinguish children's wants and needs. Children are often unaware of their needs, but they always know what they want. If parents just satisfy children's wishes, then the children will be the ones deciding what is good for them, something for which they are of course not ready. We must know when we need to say "no," but not, of course, denying the child's basic needs for food, clothing, footwear, health, sleep, love, and social relations.

The next important thing is consistency. If you are consistent, the child will know that the boundaries cannot be negotiated at different times and places. This does not mean, of course, that you should be rigid, sometimes it is also necessary to be flexible, especially if the child gives a good argument - so that they know that we respect their opinion.

Rebellion against the rules

When we say no, children may become disappointed, sad, or angry, and begin to cry. This is a normal way for children to respond to frustration and it is a necessary part of growing up. When children are angry and frustrated, we should never mock them, imitate them, blame them (from the second to the fifth year of a child's life, blame directly threatens his sense of personal worth and self-esteem), criticize, cajole, persuade them to feel guilty or to stop expressing their emotions, and especially not to change their opinion. It is necessary to accept the child's feelings, to sympathize with them, to help them to direct their emotions and to remain consistent.

It is important to not give in when a child is pleading, crying, yelling, or in any way rebelling against the rules that you set. If we give in, the child will learn to use that kind of behavior when they want something and the next time they will resort to it again. If they learn from their family that everything will go the way they want whenever they cry, scream, or throw themselves on the floor, they will use the same kind of behavior in kindergarten and that will make it much more difficult for the child to socialize.

When setting the boundaries, it is necessary to ensure that the child is heard and understood, so it is best to sit down with them, look them in the eyes and say what you want in a simple and clear way that is understandable to them. You should never promise or threaten what you cannot fulfill. Don't give up because of the child's pressure ("Please, only this time!"), because normally this will demonstrate to the child that you didn't think out what you said. If you want to be flexible, do it before your child requests something.

The best thing in the world – a hug!

Researchers once decided to collect evidence to show that parental affection benefits the welfare of children during their childhood but in their research they found that kisses and hugs from mom and dad mean even more than they thought. Scientists believe that greater self-confidence, better communication between parents and children, and less psychological and behavioral problems are linked to the warmth and attachment between parents and the child. This is one of the most important foundations of a parent-child relationship: tenderness, warmth, understanding, and trust.

Do you feel your stress and exhaustion disappear when after a long day at work you come home and hug and kiss your little ones? Children also feel that love and affection. On the other hand, researchers have found that neglecting a child, which is linked to reduced attachment and love, can affect the child's physical and mental health for life, leading to negative consequences such as poor health. We know that children, regardless of their culture, need to feel loved. Children "absorb" the meaning of what their mothers and fathers are trying to do for them.

Can you overdo love? Yes, sure you can. But there is a solution - be moderate.

In child raising, setting personal limits is just as important as understanding, love, and support. When there are limits, children learn that they are responsible for what is happening to them, it helps them learn to self-regulate their feelings and behaviors, and helps them to be self-confident, but also to gain a sense of security and trust in their parents. These are all very important skills that enable the child to achieve better success in school, and also to establish contact with peers and build friendships. Numerous studies show that an educational style in which support, acceptance, warmth and love are shown, and also in which there is a clear and consistent setting of boundaries and structure, and in which expectations are high, enables children to grow into self-confident, stable, and successful people who cultivate quality relationships with others.

Why is it important for a child to learn how to cope with feelings of frustration, sadness, and anger?

Because if they do not, they can expect problems later in life. Solving tasks will be too demanding and uninteresting, and tasks will become an obstacle. That's why it's important to do a good job with your child. When your toddler becomes frustrated or angry because he has failed to do something well, let him express his feelings because it is completely natural. You can tell your toddler: "You were really angry when your tower collapsed," or "You are very angry because I do not want to buy you another ice cream," which shows that we understand and accept the child's feelings. Beyond that, it's important not to get involved in this natural process.

Children are not born with a knowledge of what is good and what is not. These are skills that must be learned with the help of their parents. True, it's a difficult job and children need the outward support of adults. The smaller they are, the more leadership they need. But in order for them to grow, you must give them more opportunities to practice self-control.

Self-regulation refers to the ability to align one's own emotions and behaviors with the demands of one's environment and to naturally mature with time, but for the child's development, the support and guidance of adults is very important. This support consists of the way in which we accept the child and his or her feelings and the way we set the limits on unacceptable behavior.

Although at first it may seem that children are happy when they get everything they want - the opposite is actually true. The setting of clear and consistent boundaries teaches the child to be truly happy because with such an approach the child will feel safe and self-confident, and will have developed self-control. And those who are responsible for leading the child and setting up the structure have grown by respecting the child's dignity.

In order to have the boundaries that we set make a positive impact on the emotional and social development of the child, the way in which these boundaries are set up is extremely important – they need to be set up clearly, consistently, and without punishment.

When setting boundaries, a key step is to respect the child's needs and feelings. When children have difficulty controlling emotions, describing the emotions to them is the first step to teach a child about what's happening to them. For example,

"You were very angry because you couldn't watch the cartoon anymore and you hit me. But I don't want to be hit because that hurts me."

Set boundaries by telling what is acceptable to you and what is not, what you like and what you don't like. Using personal speech is much more important to the child then setting general limits. For example: "I don't like when you shout in my ear and I want you to stop" rather than "You must not shout loudly." Always be consistent. Once you set a limit, stick to the rules because in that way the child learns that he can trust you in every situation.

In order for the limit to make sense to a child, you must explain to them a consequence. The most common consequences are natural consequences, that is, those related to what the child is doing. For example, if the child continues to play with the ball in the room after you have told him or her not to, the natural consequence is that you take the ball away. Do this without raising your voice. Simply put the ball away and tell your child that the apartment is not the place for such a type of game and that he can take the ball with him when you go out to the park.

A child who is out of control needs a patient and quiet parent. If a parent loses control when a child behaves badly, and starts yelling, the little one usually responds with an outburst of anger and the problem is doubled. Keep in mind that a child is just learning important life skills and that you will best help him if you stay calm.

It is known that a lack of clear boundaries often leads to behavioral problems, so it is important to start creating healthy boundaries while children are still small. It is natural for children to try to push the limits and rules as they develop their own understanding of themselves and learn how the world works.

Parents who provide limits for their children help them to develop moral principles that will enable them to live independently once they leave the parental nest. The goal of setting good limits is for the child to achieve self-control. Self-control, in turn, develops a solid character and an inner moral compass that further leads children to think well and be honest.

Whenever possible, guide your child by positive statements, and demand the behaviors that you want the child to repeat, rather than emphasizing the behaviors you do not want. Well-established boundaries focus on the positive outcome of the child's cooperation - they should be placed as a promise, not as a threat. Setting the boundaries introduces a routine into the lives of children, and a routine provides benefits and security as they then know what to expect and when to expect it.

The boundaries should be set with as few negative emotions as possible. When a parent communicates calmly and clearly, there is less likelihood of the child being defiant. Children are perfect mirrors that reflect both positive and negative emotions. They usually do exactly what the parents themselves do, reflecting their aggravated state, not what they say. When parents consistently adhere to the boundaries and the consequences they have set, then children can more easily learn to respect others, build better self-control, develop the ability to tolerate frustration, and take responsibility for their actions.

Differences between boundaries, orders, and rules

Setting limits allows you to avoid conflicts between parent and child, while commands are based on penalties and negative consequences. Well-established boundaries are not based on the child's fear of the parent nor the fear of anger and punishment. They allow a child to experience positive and negative consequences in a safe environment of unconditional parental love. Also, such limits allow children to be responsible for their own behavior.

A child should not be blackmailed or threatened. It is better to praise them and allow some privileges for desirable and acceptable behavior. If a child behaves inappropriately and improperly, it is also very important to be sure that the child knows what about this behavior was unacceptable before a certain privilege is taken away. Taking away a privilege must never mean taking away parental love or hindering the satisfaction of the child's developmental and emotional needs.

Children need guidance and direction in order to adopt family values, and the parents are the ones who make this possible. Parents provide a barrier between a child and the improper values which come at them from all sides, and parents take the responsibility for the child by setting clear, concrete, and well-defined boundaries which they stand behind firmly. After all, you can't play a game if you don't know the rules. Boundaries are most effective when are put in place in an atmosphere of love, acceptance, and mutual respect.

Conclusion

And here we come to the end of the road. Correction, it's the end of the book. The road is just starting for you. Creativity is something within you and you're the master of it so learn to use it correctly. The real beauty of art is that there is no manual for it, no set of rules you have to follow, no one to tell you what to do. You are meant to do it your way.

Create whatever your heart desires and don't be ashamed of your work, no matter what it is. You created it because you wanted to and that is reason enough for it to exist. Even though I did say that creativity is in all humans, only a few have that side in bright lights while the others locked it in behind walls and bars. Being a creative type of person guarantees that you will be misunderstood a lot through your life, most won't see the bigger picture of what you're trying to create and even more of them will laugh at your face because they think your ideas are stupid. Don't mind them; just keep doing what you love.

Learn your craft, master it, so that when you show your work to the world you even make the haters short of breath. You can do it. With hard work and dedication, you can achieve anything. Combine that with love and care and you've got yourself a recipe for a happy life and that's all that matters in the end. Not how many books you published, what the critics said, did your painting enter the art gallery, is your song on the radio, is your sculpture somewhere in the city, none of that matters at the end of the day.

What truly matters is that, when the day finally ends and you recall of all the things you did that day, your head touches your pillow with a smile on your face. And when you wake up in the morning all groggy and sleepy, go outside on your terrace, balcony or through your window and greet the world with a defiant smile on your face. Why? Because you can. Because you, my friend, are an artist. You are – a creator.

www.ingramcontent.com/pod-product-compliance
Lightning Source LLC
Chambersburg PA
CBHW072006070526
44583CB00015B/1356